THE RECOLLECTED
HEART

The whole spectrum of what retreat means—its holy uses as well as its methods and articulation—is more fully explored, and more completely conveyed, in this small book than in any other contemporary one I know of. It is not lost on most of us that the brevity of *The Rule of St. Benedict*, from which Zaleski's manual depends, is lauded almost as much and as frequently as is its satisfying completeness. There is good reason to consider that fact here as well.

Phyllis Tickle, compiler of *The Divine Hours*

This guide to slowing down for a little while was powerful when it first appeared in 1995. But that was before the Internet took hold, before the cellphone became ubiquitous, before we walked down city streets texting as we went. Now, in 2009, it's almost a mandatory read.

Bill McKibben, author of *Deep Economy*

In *Out of Africa*, Isak Dinesen tells of arriving early with her guide for an appointment. Then follows this memorable line: "Two human beings sat down under a tree—one to wait, the other to live." Reading Philip Zaleski's *The Recollected Heart* made me want to drop everything and head for the hills to recover my capacity to truly live. It is a wonderful book, in its diction and well-crafted phrases to be sure, but more importantly in what Zaleski uses his words to say.

Huston Smith, author of *The World's Religions*

Phil Zaleski's guidelines for making a spiritual retreat are rooted in an awareness of the Divine and in his sense of the human need for respite. His tone is companionable, and he is respectful of our varying personalities and needs. A first-class handbook.

Barry Lopez, author of *Arctic Dreams* and *Crossing Open Ground*

On retreat, one finds the luxury that hides within simplicity, the power that lives within obedience, and the rich eloquence that silence contains. Philip Zaleski's pure-hearted and companionable book is a call to the best adventure of the soul that many of us have found. The more people who read it and respond to its summons, the saner and happier our world will be.

Pico Iyer, author of *The Open Road*

With skill, tact, reverence, and enormous creative imagination Philip Zaleski has done what I would have thought to be impossible: he has actually established the atmosphere of a powerful monastic retreat weekend within the pages of a book.

Rev. Andrew M. Greeley, author of *The Catholic Imagination*

What we call spiritual journeys can easily become spiritual meanderings without the good company of someone like Philip Zaleski who reminds us of the destination—and the discipline necessary to getting there.

Rev. Richard John Neuhaus, editor of *First Things*

Why do we need retreats? "To gain perspective, and to pray," writes Philip Zaleski. One grants the other, and neither is possible without a time apart. With warmth and understanding, *The Recollected Heart* encourages, guides, and supports the reader through all aspects of this essential process.

Lorraine Kisly, author of *The Prayer of Fire*

THE RECOLLECTED
HE*A*RT

A Guide to Making a Contemplative
Weekend Retreat

PHILIP ZALESKI

ave maria press **AmP** notre dame, indiana

TO CAROL

© 1995, 2009 by Philip Zaleski

Founded in 1865, Ave Maria Press is a ministry of the Indiana
Province of Holy Cross.
www.avemariapress.com

ISBN-10 1-59471-199-2   ISBN-13 978-1-59471-199-2
Cover and text design by Katherine Robinson Coleman.
Cover images iStockphoto, and Photos.com
Printed and bound in the United States of America.

Library of Congress Cataloging-in-Publication Data
Zaleski, Philip.
  The recollected heart : a guide to making a contemplative week-
end retreat /
Philip Zaleski. -- Rev. ed.
      p. cm.
  Includes bibliographical references and index.
  ISBN-13: 978-1-59471-199-2
  ISBN-10: 1-59471-199-2
 1. Spiritual retreats. I. Title.

  BX2375.A3Z35 2009
  269'.6--dc22

                                        2008047927

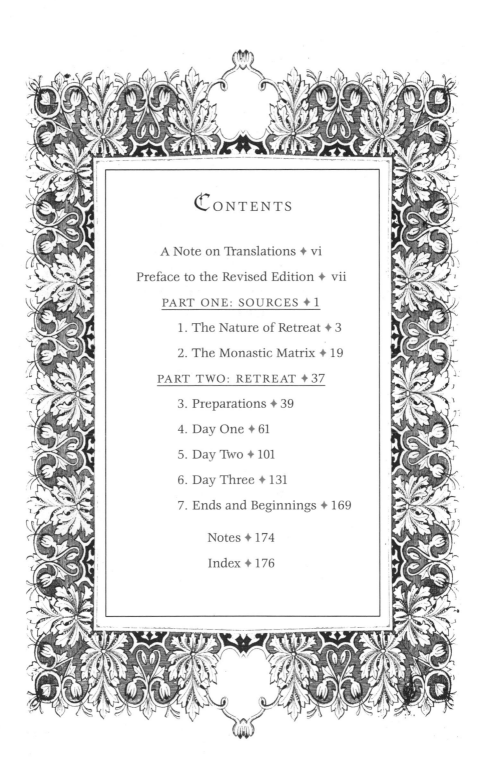

CONTENTS

$\mathcal{A}$ NOTE ON TRANSLATIONS

Most biblical quotations in the text come from the New Revised Standard Version Bible (copyright 1989, Division of Christian Education of the National Council of the Churches of Christ in the United States of America. Used by permission. All rights reserved.) However, very occasionally I have turned to other translations in order to highlight the traditional meaning of a particular teaching or event. These translations include the Revised Standard Version Bible (copyright 1946, 1952, 1971, Division of Christian Education of the Churches of Christ in the United States of America) and the Authorized Version (King James Version). All such instances are noted in the text.

All quotations from St. Benedict's *Rule* come from *RB 1980: The Rule of St. Benedict in Latin and English with Notes* (Collegeville, MN: Liturgical Press, 1981).

The translation of two stanzas of Dante's *Paradiso* is by Carol Zaleski.

℘REFACE TO THE REVISED EDITION

Forty years ago, the typical educated American (that wholly fictitious but useful figure) knew, about the Benedictines, two things: that their schools were good and that their liqueur was better. Twenty years ago, thanks to a best-selling compact disc by the Spanish monks of Santo Domingo dc Silos, Gregorian chant was added to this scant store of knowledge. Today things remain the same. Now, it's true that Benedictines excel at drink, song, and learning—vital aspects of monastic life addressed by St. Benedict in his *Rule*—but the Benedictine ethos is much larger than this. To demonstrate how much larger is, in a way, the aim of the book you hold in your hands.

If pressed, I might say that to discover the Benedictine world is to discover . . . just about everything. Read the *Rule*, and you will find the laws of a joyous, well-regulated, fulfilling life. Ponder the Benedictine vows, and you will learn the Christian meaning of stability, obedience, conversion, hospitality, and many another practice and virtue. Work like a Benedictine, and you will unearth the intimate relation between labor and faith. Pray like a Benedictine, and you may discover, with God's grace, the way to God.

vii

Last weekend, I drove the familiar route through the pine-clad hills of western Massachusetts to visit the Benedictine monasteries of Petersham, Massachusetts, the twin communities described in this book. It had been a month since my last visit, and already it seemed too long. I first visited St. Mary's Monastery and St. Scholastica Priory in 1990; during the many years that have passed since then, they have become the bedrock upon which my family and I have anchored our spiritual life. Some of the faces at St. Mary's and St. Scholastica have changed, the library has moved, the bakery has closed, a lovely new church now occupies the sward between the two communities. But underneath these alterations the essential remains: a life of prayer, study, and manual labor, consecrated to God under the guidance of St. Benedict and his *Rule*.

Recently I've had the chance to revisit *The Recollected Heart*, too, in order to prepare this revised edition for Ave Maria Press. I've made changes in the text, tightening the prose here, clarifying ideas there, adding and subtracting in keeping with my present understanding of Benedictine life. But the essence of the book, like that of the communities that inspire it, remains the same. I still believe that prayer, in its many modes of petition, thanksgiving, adoration, and contemplation, is among the highest, most beautiful, and most arduous of human occupations, one in which the struggle is commensurate with the reward (and often the struggle is the reward). I still believe that the Benedictine life is nothing less than a majestic prayer enunciated by the whole person: body, mind, heart, and spirit. I still believe that this life can be tasted, if not fully assimilated, during a three-day retreat. And I still believe that, as soon as one comes into contact with Benedictine monasticism, a door opens onto the entire Christian tradition—scripture, liturgy, art, good works, and, above all, the love and saving grace of Jesus Christ.

I'd like to offer, for this revised edition, a new set of acknowledgments. First and foremost, my warmest thanks to the Benedictine monks and nuns of Petersham, without whom this book would have been impossible. I owe a particular debt to Right Rev. Anselm Atkinson, O.S.B., Superior of St. Mary's Monastery and Abbot-Visitor of the English Province of the Subiaco Congregation: a true son of St. Benedict, a scholar, and a dear friend. His poorest Hebrew student hereby acknowledges his gratitude for many hours of delightful philological discussion, ranging over the entire corpus of Near Eastern languages, and reminds him that the gates of Ugaritic still beckon. My debt to Sister Mary Clare Vincent, O.S.B., former prioress of St. Scholastic Priory, is scarcely less; she exemplifies in her leadership, kindness, and musical gifts all that makes Benedictines justly loved.

I wish also to express my gratitude to others who have helped me, through advice or inspiration, in the creation of this book in its original or present form, among them Stratford and Léonie Caldecott; Rt. Rev. Hugh Gilbert, O.S.B., Abbot of Pluscarden; Rev. Dom Bede Kierney, O.S.B.; and Msgr. Daniel P. Liston. My thanks also to Annie Dillard, who recommended so many years ago that I undertake this project; and to Tom Grady and all the folks at Ave Maria Press for inviting me to prepare this revised edition. Finally, my deepest thanks to Carol, John, and Andy for giving me, now and always, the best reason in the world to come back from retreat.

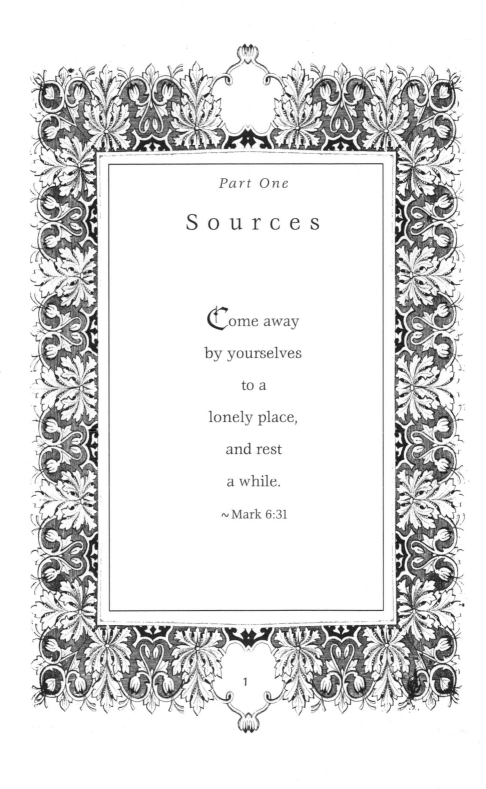

Part One

Sources

Come away

by yourselves

to a

lonely place,

and rest

a while.

~ Mark 6:31

*T*HE NATURE OF RETREAT

Several years ago, I found myself in the strange and comical situation, as the ancient Middle Eastern saying has it, of "trying to jump over my own knees." A major decision loomed, one whose consequences would shake every pillar of my life. I fretted over my possibilities, I fiddled and fussed. Try as I might, I couldn't make a final choice. Plans A, C, E, and G pointed to failure, along a spectrum ranging from discomfort to catastrophe. Options B, D, and F promised success, but they entailed sacrifices that I felt unwilling to make. I was bewildered, half-beaten, queasy in my soul. Well-meaning friends gave me conflicting advice: to leap forward, to back-paddle, to give up. Books proved to be another dead end: the first steered me north; the next, due south. What to do?

To break the stalemate, I went on retreat. I borrowed a friend's cabin up in the New Hampshire woods, a rustic affair at the end of an unmarked dirt road, with night crawlers in the basement and bats in the attic. The nearest neighbors ran a small dairy farm a half mile to the south. To the north rose the rocky face of Mt. Washington, New England's tallest peak, where a few decades ago meteorologists had measured the strongest winds on record, whipping the weather vanes at 231 miles per hour. Although I never climbed the mountain, for the span of my exile I felt like I was standing on the summit with those hurricane winds roaring through my soul. For five days I was cut off, cut loose; I was *away*: atop the world, light-years from Earth, gazing back like some distant astronaut on our little green-and-blue ball of life. Blessed Julian of Norwich's vision flashed into my mind, of the time that God had presented her with the world:

> He showed me something small, no bigger than a hazelnut, lying in the palm of my hand, and I perceived that it was as round as any ball. I looked at it and thought: What can this be? And I was given this general answer: It is everything which is made. I was amazed that it could last, for I thought that it was so little that it could suddenly fall into nothing. And I was answered in my understanding: It lasts and always will, because God loves it; and thus everything has being through the love of God.[1]

Ralph Waldo Emerson had a similar experience:

> I dreamed that I floated at will in the great Ether, and I saw this world floating also not far off, but diminished to the size of an apple. Then an angel took it in his hand and brought it to me and said, "This must thou eat." And I ate the world.[2]

Visionary nuns and dreaming poets: what better guides for my retreat? Reason had failed to answer my dilemma; perhaps in vapors and chimeras I would find what I sought. But I wasn't ready just yet to eat the world. I was savoring abstinence, the sudden escape from my regular feast of gossip and "news." No newspapers, magazines, or TV broadcasts intruded upon me during those few days of retreat. And this privation—which from the first I knew would be a blessing—proved to be only the beginning. A deeper solitude was mine. No human beings crossed my path—no inquisitive neighbors, no friends who "just heard you were alone and stopped by to make sure that you were okay." No letters, telegrams, or phone calls invaded my mountain aerie. No one knew where I was; I might have been on Mars. I tipped my cap to grazing sheep on my morning stroll and accepted a nuzzle from my neighbor's cow on my after-dinner constitutional. Apart from these happy salutations, I was utterly alone.

Soon after arriving at my country cabin, I sat down to smoke a pipeful of cherry tobacco (today, I'd be content to chew a wad of gum) and contemplate the pinkish-grey clouds curling around the Presidential peaks. I felt as snug as Crusoe tucked away in his island safe-hold, and half imagined grabbing flintlock and umbrella for a pleasant stroll along the beach. As the sky-wisps cleaved and coagulated overhead, memories flooded back of earlier times when I had gone off to be alone. I realized that retreat—this need to be with myself for a time, to make a little world within the world where I could be safe and where I could think—was a leitmotiv of my life. And so it is with everyone. We all enter the world after a good retreat, nine months in our mother's womb, in the cushioned serenity of the amniotic ocean, where the miraculous transformation from one level of being to another takes place and a clump of cells becomes a bawling baby. A comparable change, it struck me, is what we adults desire when we make for the hills. We seek rebirth in things large and small. We long to be refreshed, reseeded, reinspired, to "be renewed in the spirit," as St. Paul puts it so stirringly in his letter to the Ephesians.

As the clouds swirled, so did my mind, and memories of earlier retreats rose to consciousness. I remembered Boy Scout camp at the age of nine or ten. This summer holiday proved to be a retreat within a retreat, for the camp, pocketed deep in the woods and thus an exile from my ordinary suburban life, seemed to me a frightening place where I, a shy bookish boy more comfortable pitching an idea than a tent, knew hardly a soul and couldn't grasp the rules. So I wrangled my way into the job of troop mailboy and spent a good chunk of each day walking at a turtle's pace to the post office several miles away from our encampment, a heavenly excursion in which I could simply be myself and confront nothing more threatening that a lost backpacker or a lumbering porcupine. In this escape from camp—itself an escape from ordinary life—I first tasted the terror and bliss of solitude.

I recalled, too, times at college when I would leave my partying roommates in the smoky common room, plunge into the cold night air, and make for the hidden garden tucked behind one of the Greek revival mansions that dotted the campus, there to prop my back against a bird bath, breathe deeply, and pray. Other self-imposed enclosures came back: winter in a Vermont cabin, spring in an Istanbul hotel, summer in a Montana lodge, autumn in a Parisian apartment; retreats before births and after deaths, retreats during times of crisis and times of peace. These many periods of self-renewal taught me what to expect during my present seclusion, snuggled at the foot of the New Hampshire mountains. Certain things always happen on retreat—at least if one is properly prepared. Time slows down; space dilates. Objects attain a starkness of outline and brilliancy of color that they rarely possess in ordinary life. Things become transparent, and their essential being shines through. While on retreat, I find that when I lift a fork, I register its well-balanced weight, the elegance of its four-tined design, just right for the task at hand. When I chew a raspberry, the whole fruit rushes forth to meet me: the tiny hairs stubbling the skin, the tart juice, the rough globular joy of its raspberriness, like a red sun come down to earth.

I, too, change while on retreat. As the world comes to me, I go forth to greet it, gladly. I slow down, take my time with things, enter into each activity with all my being. When I sit, I really sit, and my weight settles into the earth. When I stand, my legs become pillars, supporting the great trunk of spine and chest, the architectonic wizardry of arms, neck, and head. When I walk, I feel the frigid air pumping into my lungs; I sense against my palms the dry scratch of woolen gloves; I hear, as a definite fracture in the fabric of silence, the crack of branches breaking underfoot. Such events shed their remoteness, their alienness. They speak to me, friend to friend, and I begin to listen.

But all this is the least of it. Away from the world's ceaseless din, I hear whispers from another realm, faint but compelling. Honed senses, vitality, other external changes—as valuable as they may be—only hint at the real metamorphosis to come. New possibilities beckon, fresh ways of seeing, doing, and being, gifts at once familiar and strange. One is *perspective*; another is *prayer*.

We all know what perspective means (but how rarely we attain it): the ability to see a situation objectively, as someone else might see it. Its importance cannot be overstated. The hunt for perspective explains not only why we go on weekend retreat, but why athletes have coaches, writers have editors, and everyone (even God, insists the Christian tradition) has a mother. On retreat, we see with new eyes, we think with new minds. We become our own counselors, and sometimes we even take our own good advice.

Even more important, however, is the advent of prayer. I say "advent" (that is, "coming" or "arrival") deliberately. Each time we pray, it is like arriving at another level of being, like swimming from stygian depths to the sunlit surface, where we float for a while in the presence of God. During my stay in the New Hampshire woods, I swam repeatedly upward, greeted the sun that burns both day and night, and laid my burden in its scorching rays. I entrusted everything, once and for all, to God. I had little in the way of theology or metaphysics to guide me; I only knew that I needed a helpmeet infinitely more wise and ancient than myself. How to act? Where to turn? I did the only thing I could do: I fell to my knees and prayed.

To attain perspective and to pray—to become self-reliant by relying on God—this is no small ambition. Many books discuss the hows and whys, and none of them get it exactly right. I know that I didn't. Sometimes during my alpine retreat I felt dizzy, in despair, on the verge of crumpling. At other times, I enjoyed the cool energies that quiet brings. For a while my plans would run smoothly, and then they would rupture beyond hope. But slowly, the fog of my confusion lifted. In time an answer came. It always does if one waits long enough and gives stillness, silence, and solitude a chance to do their work. Was I sure about my choice? No, not at all, but as G.K. Chesterton said, "If a thing is worth doing, it is worth doing badly." Chesterton, a man whose penetration into the human soul was as acute as his wit, also remarked, "I do not believe in a fate that falls on men however they act; but I do believe in a fate that falls on men unless they act." I acted; my life changed; I have had no regrets.

"Society is like the air," wrote American philosopher George Santayana, "necessary to breathe, but insufficient to live on." To find real sustenance, as I discovered on that mountainside more than a decade ago, we must at times seek a place apart. The wish to retreat from the daily bump and bustle has given rise to many a profound—or at least piquant—spiritual adventure, unfolding in caves, on mountaintops, or in a quiet corner of a busy home. I have my own list of favorites, among them Siddhartha Gautama under the bodhi tree, St. Simeon Stylites on his desert pillar, Henry Thoreau beside Walden Pond, Richard Byrd in his Antarctic dugout, reading *Walden* as the blizzards howled.

Retreat, as everyone in this company will testify, is a richly textured affair, harboring something of exploration, something of escape, and something of life-and-death struggle. Whatever the precise mix, one truth abides: retreat is neither whim nor luxury nor self-indulgence, but a rock-bottom staple of a healthy life. We need retreat as surely as we need oxygen or protein. While any given retreat may start out as a joyride—a few days away from spouse, kids, or job, a chance to spread one's wings, loosen one's belt, kick up one's heels—it always winds up as a pilgrimage. We start to look for what really counts. Thoreau states the case in this justly famous passage from *Walden*:

> I went to the woods because I wished to live deliberately, to front only the essential facts of life, and see if I could not learn what it had to teach, and not, when I came to die, discover that I had not lived. I did not wish to live what was not life, living is so dear, nor did I wish to practice resignation, unless it was quite necessary. I wanted to live deep and suck out all the marrow of life.[3]

Retreat, then, is life stripped bare, boiled to the bones, pared to first and final things. In the Christian tradition, such uncloaking of self and senses plays an indispensable role in spiritual growth. God calls us, always and everywhere; our task is to find conditions that allow us to hear and respond to the divine invitation. Breaking from habit, filtering out the noise of the world, seeking a place apart: these are good ways to begin. But during the silence that follows, where will we incline our ears? Inward, answers Jesus, for "the kingdom of God is within you" (Lk 17:21, KJV). While philosophers have cracked their heads over the nuances of this statement, few people miss its central message: we must, as St. Augustine put it, "return to the heart" and there seek God. The earliest Christians called this process "recollection," the act of remembering (re-membering, re-collecting) ourselves, God, and the love that binds us. During retreat, we stitch together, with the needle of silence and the thread of stillness, our scattered sense of self and our fragmentary experience of God.

To some, this process, with its emphasis on interior work, may sound like narcissism in the raw. Nothing could be further from the truth. Jesus' proclamation that "the kingdom of God is within you" may also be translated as "the kingdom of God is among you"—that is, in your midst and with your neighbors. Turning inward means turning outward (the spiritual life teems with such happy paradoxes). Jesus, while proclaiming through word and deed the absolute necessity for periodic retreat, nonetheless engaged in an active ministry of preaching, healing, and prophecy. Like Jesus, we, too, may find that retreat leads to deeper engagement with others. This curious motion—simultaneously inward and outward, toward myself and toward the world—lies at the heart of this Danish folk tale, relayed by Søren Kierkegaard:

> A man . . . was so tired of his home that he had his horse saddled in order to ride forth into the wide world. When he had gone a little distance, his horse threw him. This turn of events was decisive for him, for when he turned to mount his horse, his eye lit again upon the home he wished to leave and behold, it was so beautiful that he at once turned back.[4]

By going on retreat, we give ourselves the opportunity— without, one hopes, too severe a bump—to dismount, turn around, and see our life afresh. At its very best, this vision brings with it joy, energy, and a sense of purpose that revitalizes us and those around us. It may even change the world. In 1978 President Jimmy Carter, Egyptian President Anwar Sadat, and Israeli

Prime Minister Menachem Begin, devout men from different faiths, gathered at Camp David for a twelve-day conference, often punctuated by prayer, that the participants pointedly called a "retreat" and that gave birth to the acclaimed Camp David Accords, which led in turn to the 1979 Israeli-Egypt Peace Treaty. Can you imagine such a splendid outcome, of benefit to all humankind, resulting from secular, public talks in Geneva or Stockholm? Here, right conditions and right outlook made all the difference. So may it be with our own time apart.

The Camp David event tells us something else important about retreat: we needn't insist upon forty days in the wilderness. Even a three-day withdrawal from ordinary life permits serious spiritual work to begin. By the third day, we may, if we open ourselves unreservedly to God, encounter important truths that evade us in the haste and heat of ordinary life. The same flexibility applies to our choice of locale. Admiral Byrd's subterranean polar hut had its charms, including total solitude, security, and a symbolic affinity to the womb. Some Tibetan ascetics go so far as to immure themselves within a cave for life with only a narrow slit to allow the passage of food, water, and wastes. For our purposes, however, a house, apartment, cabin, tent, or monastic guest room will do just as well. I once knew a man who made an annual retreat in the Maine woods with nothing but a blanket, a book, and a good working knowledge of herbs and berries. The essential thing is to divorce ourselves as far as possible from the habits and pressures of our workaday lives. If we drag our old patterns into the retreat, we will soil our surroundings and turn our solitude into nothing more than a vacation. Some Native

Americans parboil in a sweat lodge before undertaking a vision quest; on our retreat, the same principle rules: we must wash away the old world before entering the new (this will be discussed in more detail in chapter 3). Outer and inner ablutions aside, there remains only one prerequisite: a genuine desire to bathe in the stream of God's undying love. If we settle for dipping our toes, we may enjoy a pleasant holiday from ordinary life, even bring back some picturesque snapshots of our time apart, but we can be certain that little wisdom will come our way. If we dive boldly, however, taking the plunge with all our being, we may find ourselves immersed in living waters.

The roots of Christian retreat burrow into antiquity, to the primordial retreats of Moses in the Sinai wilderness. According to the Book of Exodus, Moses' first withdrawal from the world—and his first encounter with God—came unexpectedly while he tended his sheep on Mt. Horeb. An "angel of the Lord" appeared in the form of a burning bush, a plant that never turned to ash, for it blazed with a spiritual flame. Speaking through the bush, God revealed to Moses the Divine Name, placed on his shoulders the mantle of prophecy, and promised to the Israelites deliverance from slavery. Years later, Moses again scaled the Sinai heights— this time on deliberate retreat—in order to receive the Ten Commandments, along with instructions for erecting the sacred tabernacle and the Ark of the Covenant.

What can we glean from these mountain ascents of Moses, which brought such treasures to the world? Perfect prototypes, they display the quintessential elements of all retreat:

Retreat may lead to divine gifts. During his withdrawal from the world, Moses—who here represents all human beings—opens his heart to God, and God in turn grants to Moses and his people all that they desire: a teacher, a moral code, a ritual practice, a land in which to thrive. "Take delight in the Lord, and he will give you the desires of your heart," exclaims the Hebrew Psalter (Ps 37:4).

Retreat never takes place alone. Once Moses scales the mountain, God never abandons him. So it is with us in solitude: we will never be alone. Tradition assures us, on the contrary, that always—and most emphatically while on retreat—God mantles us with love, the air throngs with angels, and saints kindly bend their heads our way.

Retreat demands special conditions and behavior. During Moses' first ascent, a voice commands him to "remove the sandals from your feet, for the place on which you are standing is holy ground" (Ex 3:5). As we climb our own more modest Sinai, we too must take appropriate measures, denuding ourselves of encumbrances, stripping ourselves bare in the presence of holiness.

According to Christian teaching, the great retreats of Moses and other Hebrew prophets—Abraham, Isaac, Jacob, so many generations of seers that they make the head spin—lead in "the fullness of time" to those undertaken by God Incarnate, Jesus Christ. The New Testament abounds with references to Jesus' retreats and to his counsels on the subject: Jesus "got up and went out to a deserted place, and there he prayed" (Mk 1:35); Jesus instructs his disciples to "come away to a deserted place all by yourselves and rest a while" (Mk

6:31); Jesus tells us, in the Sermon on the Mount, that "whenever you pray, go into your room and shut the door and pray to your Father who is in secret" (Mt 6:5).

These varied prescriptions are epitomized by Jesus' withdrawal into the desert immediately following his baptism: "Jesus, full of the Holy Spirit, returned from the Jordan and was led by the Spirit in the wilderness" (Lk 4:1–2). Here, alone for forty days, he engages in spiritual combat, overcoming three temptations offered by the devil: to change stone into bread, to rule the earth, to plummet from a mountain and be saved by angels; these present, in dramatic form, the three great temptations that we encounter on the spiritual path: indulgence, power, and pride. Upon his triumphal return from these trials, Jesus reads in the synagogue at Nazareth the following messianic passage from Isaiah:

> The Spirit of the Lord is upon me because he has anointed me to bring good news to the poor. He has sent me to proclaim release to the captives and recovery of sight to the blind, to let the oppressed go free, to proclaim the year of the Lord's favor. (Lk 4:18–19)

In time, the retreats of Moses and Jesus became paradigms for those of Western monasticism. Centers of religious formation sprang up—first in Egypt and Syria, then in Europe and, eventually, Asia and the Americas—where men and women struggled mightily and sometimes successfully to overcome their fallen nature and become sons and daughters of God. Consider, for example, the fourth-century retreat of St. Antony of the Desert, the prototypical Christian monk, who secreted himself inside a ruined fortress for—this seems impossible but the text insists upon it—twenty years. *The Life of Antony* by St. Athanasius describes the saint as he emerges from his solitude:

> The state of his soul was one of purity, for it was not constricted by grief, nor relaxed by pleasure, nor affected by either laughter or dejection. . . . When he saw the crowd, he was not annoyed any more than he was elated at being embraced by so many people. He maintained utter equilibrium, like one guided by reason and steadfast in that which accords with nature. Through him the Lord healed many of those present who suffered from bodily ailments. . . . He consoled many who mourned, and others hostile to each other he reconciled in friendship.[5]

In his courage, compassion, and serenity, Antony serves as a model for all who seek the treasures of the heart. Over the centuries, innumerable ascetics have followed his example—albeit usually without becoming cave-bound hermits for twenty years. For a less strenuous form of Christian retreat suited to our frail modern constitutions, we might look at the example set by St. Augustine, who shortly after his conversion in 387 sequestered himself with his mother, St. Monica, in a villa at Ostia at the mouth of the Tiber River. There, he writes in his *Confessions*, "our conversation was serene and joyful." He continues with a radiant description of the blessings of retreat, this time enjoyed by two people in unison (the *you* in the following passage refers to God; Augustine, with his characteristic blend of humility and audacity, addresses his autobiography—the first in world literature and still the best—directly to his Maker):

> As the flame of love burned stronger in us and raised us higher toward the eternal God, our thoughts ranged over the whole compass of material things in their various degrees, up to the heavens themselves, from which the sun and the moon and the stars shine down upon the earth. Higher still we climbed, thinking and speaking all the while in wonder at all that you have made. . . . And while we spoke of the eternal Wisdom, longing for it and straining for it with all the strength of our hearts, for one fleeting instant we reached out and touched it.[6]

Not all retreats unfold under such sunny conditions. Witness the imprisonments of St. John of the Cross (1542–1591) and John Bunyan (1628–1688). In each case, years in solitary confinement—involuntary retreat, one is tempted to call it, while wincing at the impertinence—led to profound spiritual insights and, not incidentally, some great religious poetry and prose. Or consider St. Catherine of Siena (1347–1380), who spent three years as a teenager in self-imposed isolation, a self-immolation that led to a "mystical marriage to Christ" as well as to her most important book, *The Dialogue*, which takes Augustine's literary temerity one step further, for in it God addresses the reader in the first person. Nor do idiosyncratic Christian withdrawals from the world grind to a halt in modern times; thus John Henry Newman in the stables of Littlemore, Abhishiktananda in the mountains of northern India, Annie Dillard on the banks of Tinker Creek.

These many examples underscore the diversity of retreat. Jesus slept in the open air, Antony a rotting garrison, Newman a converted horse shed, Dillard a cabin. While Augustine and his mother shared a roof, most retreatants choose to be alone. Sometimes,

however, these preferences come to naught: many soli-
taries attract followers who bunk down alongside them
willy-nilly. Some retreats precede great events, as an
anticipatory gathering of spiritual energies, while others come as an aftermath, a chance to reflect after the
dust has settled. Retreats vary in content as well as
form. We can never anticipate what will happen. Our
time apart may overturn a lifetime of convictions or it
may confirm our fondest beliefs. Whatever our experience, we do well to keep in mind the grand procession
of men and women who have preceded us. The
moment that we decide to withdraw from the world,
however brief our retreat, however hesitant our
resolve, we forge a new link in a great chain of
retreatants stretching back across millennia to the
ancient Israelites; we join in a common enterprise with
Moses and all his spiritual progeny. Once again, the
truth obtains: on retreat, we are never alone.

ᴄHE MONASTIC MATRIX

The little chapel sleeps. Sunlight pours through the floor-to-ceiling windows. Outside, a stone statue of the Virgin oversees the garden: in winter, Our Lady of the Snows, a white bonnet on her frosty head; in summer, Our Lady of the Flowers, encircled by a sea of blossoms. In every season, birds alight and sing on her weathered shoulders. Inside the chapel, however, silence rules. A scattering of people dot the pews, kneeling or sitting. Occasionally, someone turns a page in a prayer book, releasing a thin, dry rustling that echoes against the white-washed walls. Otherwise all is quiet, all is stillness. The room waits.

Then comes change, infinitesimal at first, a slight trembling in the quality of the silence. The air shimmers with anticipation. The tread of feet can be heard far in the distance, growing stronger as it nears.

Suddenly a wave of black surges into the room, a great ebony crest of water—or so it seems at first. But this is a human inundation, a line of women dressed in black, black veils on black robes, black books in hand, so much black against the sun-splashed walls that it confounds the eye. The women flow into the chapel, two abreast, and the congregation rises as one: it is impossible to sit through an event like this, which feels a bit like a parade, a bit like a funeral, and a lot like a royal procession. Then the nuns break into song, and it is as if heaven has flung open its shutters to let out the music. The Gregorian chant lilts and purls, soars and dips like a bird coasting on the winds of God. As the nuns approach the altar, they bow two by two, turn left and file into their choir stalls. Just then, as the high trill of the female voices thrills the spine, a deeper, rolling note appears. Behind the nuns emerge larger forms, also garbed in black, without veils but bearded: the monks have arrived. They, too, bow toward the altar—making, like the nuns, a full bend from the waist, head dipping as low as possible—then turn right and proceed to their respective stalls. Now nuns and monks face one another, voices merged in song. Chant bathes the chapel, saturates the walls, floods the pews. The Mass has begun.

This scene repeats itself every day of the year in Petersham, Massachusetts, home of the twin communities of St. Scholastica Priory (for women) and St. Mary's Monastery (for men). Here live some of the happiest human beings I know. These monks and nuns suffer the same agonies as other people: rejection, frustration, fear, failure, and so on. But underneath their troubles and sins runs a current of pure joy, like a cold, clean river beneath a city, and everyone senses its presence.

I go on retreat here whenever I can, which is never as often as I would like. I stay in the guesthouse, dropping my bags in a spartan room containing nothing but a bed, a battered table and chair, and a crucifix. I spend hours in this room. Here I read, sleep, pray, meditate, fret, rejoice, pass the time alone with God. I eat with the monks, participate in the liturgy, wander in the woods. But always I come back to this room. The first time I saw its four bare walls, I was terrified. What should I expect? How should I behave? *What was I doing here?*

I needn't have worried. As I might have guessed, I was in capable hands. The monks and nuns assuaged my worries, broke through my stupidities, and taught me, mostly by example, a little bit about what retreat can offer. Their presence confirmed my intuition that in matters of the spirit, we do well to rely on experienced guides, those who have surveyed the peaks and valleys before us and can navigate the landscape blindfolded if need be. In many religions (especially Christianity, Buddhism, and Hinduism), such expertise concentrates in monasteries among men and women who have devoted their adult lives to spiritual search. But I've learned also that one needn't be on site to taste the fruits of the monastic way. Christian monastic practices adapt themselves readily to a retreat by oneself or with others beyond abbey walls. Some share of the wisdom of nuns and monks can be ours as well, no matter where, when, or under what conditions we choose to go on retreat.

This chapter is titled "The Monastic Matrix." Those with a taste for etymology will recognize *matrix* as a late Latin word meaning "womb," deriving from *mater*, or "mother." Over the years many ordinary people have found monasticism to be just that: mother to spiritual life of every kind and degree. One reason that monastic practices have proven so fertile is their simplicity. As we will see, they draw on the plainest, most common activities—sitting, singing, reading, chopping carrots, or folding laundry—transforming each (ideally) into a discipline of exquisite beauty and profundity. Every aspect of our three-day retreat, from general comportment to specific prayers, springs from the womb of Western monasticism. Modifications have been introduced when necessary, but the monastic inspiration remains secure.

Most Christian monasteries adhere to the *Rule of St. Benedict*; that is to say, they follow basic precepts of a way of life first set down by St. Benedict of Nursia in the Italian hills some fifteen hundred years ago. To this day, Benedictinism remains the most widespread Christian monastic form. Its influence has spilled far beyond its own walls, for a number of other monastic orders (such as the Cistercians, to which Thomas Merton belonged) are variations on the Benedictine theme. Benedictine houses abound in the Catholic Church, with hundreds of monasteries spread across every continent except Antarctica; Anglican, Lutheran, and ecumenical, non-denominational Benedictine monasteries also flourish around the globe. In addition, tens of thousands of laypeople have struck spiritual bedrock by formally affiliating themselves with a Benedictine monastery through a process known as oblation.

It's not difficult to fathom the source of Benedict's enormous influence. His teaching shines with compassion and common sense. He treasures those things that never tarnish: learning, prayer, hospitality. As such, Benedictine monasteries have proven to be invaluable centers of peace and sanctity, particularly in times of social turmoil. In Louis Malle's delightful 1980 film *My Dinner with André*, theater director André Gregory describes Benedictine monasteries during such epochs (for instance, AD 600–900 in Europe) as "islands of safety where history can be remembered and the human being can continue to function, in order to maintain the species through a Dark Age"; the mission of these oases, he says, is "to preserve the light, life, the culture."[1] André, who relishes apocalyptic diagnoses, believes that modern society is enshrouding itself in just such a Dark Age. I am inclined toward a sunnier view but agree with him that in our very stressful time—as in every era—monasteries and monastic retreat remain invaluable, perhaps even indispensable, for all who value the spiritual life.

In a sense, the monks and nuns of Petersham, Massachusetts, have hunkered down to a permanent retreat. All Benedictines make three promises upon donning the black habit. The first is *stability*: the monk or nun pledges to remain rooted (i.e., to remain in retreat) for the rest of his or her life in the particular monastery where he or she lives. This can be a formidable discipline, especially in a nation like the United States, where John and Jane Doe switch residences, on average, once every eight years. At its most austere, in the case of cloistered communities, it means never leaving the enclosed grounds except under special circumstances. In former days, and in the few remaining monasteries that practice strict enclosure—a special privilege granted to those communities suited for it—bars crisscross the windows, and those (particularly women) who choose the consecrated life address their infrequent visitors across an iron grille. These impressive security arrangements exist, it has been said, not to lock in the monks and nuns but to lock out the profane world. Within their enclosure, Benedictines find an exhilarating freedom, one that comes from dropping the demands of the ego in order to learn, as Abbot Denis Huerre, O.S.B., puts it, how to "breathe with God's own breath."[2]

The second Benedictine promise is that of "obedience," especially to the head monk, or abbot (from Aramaic *abba*, "father"), who "holds the place"—Benedict's term—of Christ in the monastery. In asking for this pledge, so inflammatory to modern ears, Benedict doesn't mean abject surrender to the abbot's every whim, but rather exactly the action that Abbot Huerre describes above: breaking the chains of self-love and substituting in their stead the unfettered love of God. Through obedience, the monk dies to self-will to be reborn in conformity to the will of God. As the earliest proto-monks of the Egyptian desert discovered, such obedience turns death to life, barrenness to abundance:

> They told this story of Abba John the Short. He went to an old man from the Thebaid who was living in the desert of Scete. His abba once took a dead stick and planted it, and told him: "Pour a jug of water over its base every day until it bears fruit." Water was so far from their cell that he went away to fetch it every evening and did not return until dawn. At the end of three years the stick turned green, and bore fruit. The old man picked some of the fruit and took it to church, and said to the brothers, "Take and eat the fruit of obedience."[3]

The old man is each of us; the stick, our soul; the planting, obedience; the water, discipline; the fruit, renewal through love. But by what means can we know how or when or where to plant and tend our stick, especially we who live outside of monasteries? How can we discover the will of God? The best answer that I have heard to this crucial question, around which the entire monastic life revolves, came from Fr. Anselm Atkinson, superior at St. Mary's Monastery. "The will of God," he said to me, "is other people." We discern God's will—God's loving intention for his creation—by turning away from ourselves and toward others (thus the renowned Benedictine emphasis on hospitality). By seeking the other, I find myself; by heeding the other, I heal myself.

For the third promise, Benedict uses the Latin term *conversatio morum suorum*, an idiomatic expression whose original meaning has been lost (literally, the words read as "the way of life of his behavior," an opaque expression at best). To circumvent this problem, for hundreds of years monks—showing quite exceptional cunning—have transcribed the phrase with *"conversio"* in place of *"conversatio."* This tiny change solves the dilemma, for the retailored phrase means "conversion of manners," or simply "conversion." In spite of its dubious provenance, this reading has become standard, a perfect example of the practicality and plasticity of the Benedictine way. As in the case of obedience, the meaning of "conversion" (or *conversio*, as Benedictines everywhere refer to it) runs deeper than may at first appear. It has nothing to do with our very modern notion of choosing one religion or another to follow; writing in the fifth century, Benedict took it for granted that his monks would be Christian; he would be startled, and I think delighted, by the multitude of non-Christians (especially, in the last few decades, Buddhists) who have pored over his *Rule* with pleasure. Indeed for Benedict, *conversio* means something absolutely vital to real spiritual growth: the ever-renewed, ever-vigilant, continuous turning from ourselves to God. Together, the three promises of stability, obedience, and *conversio* define the Benedictine way. They will play a major role on our retreat.

Appropriately enough, Benedict's teaching itself came about through a retreat, one of the most celebrated in Christian history. It took place during the first decades of the sixth century as classical Roman civilization, a thousand years old, crumbled under the assault of foreign invasions. Visigoths, Vandals, and Huns hammered at the Eternal City's doors; blood flowed, disease rampaged, chaos reigned. Into this environment Benedict was born (ca. 480) in Nursia, a small town some forty miles south of Rome. While still a young man, he heard the call to holiness and withdrew to a rocky grotto in the Anio Valley north of Rome, overlooking an artificial lake built by Nero. Here Benedict passed three years in isolation, clad in animal skins, keeping silence, sustained by bread that a local peasant lowered to him on a rope.

Benedict's reputation for holiness soon spread. A priest approached him, then shepherds, then members of a nearby monastery, begging him to become their abbot. Benedict agreed, but the men rebelled at his severe regime (although, as we will see, it was rather moderate) and tried to poison him with tainted wine. Not surprisingly, Benedict retreated to his grotto. Here, he redoubled his efforts in self-discipline and prayer, as St. Gregory the Great reports:

> Blessed Benedict . . . can be said to have lived "within himself" because at all times he kept such

close watch over his life and actions. By searching continually into his own soul he always beheld himself in the presence of his Creator.[4]

If Benedict had remained in his cave, the history of Western civilization would have been vastly different. Happily, other monks soon petitioned the hermit for assistance, and before long Benedict had established a dozen new monasteries, each composed of twelve monks and an abbot (based, of course, upon the apostolic model). Eventually, Benedict himself became abbot at Monte Cassino, a monastery erected on the site of a temple of Apollo, eighty miles south of Rome. The monastery stands to this day, albeit rebuilt from scratch after Allied planes pounded it to rubble during World War II. There, according to Gregory, Benedict performed a number of miracles, such as expelling demons, instantly knitting broken bones, and foretelling the destruction of Rome. More enduringly, there he wrote his *Rule*.

We might fairly call the *Rule* Benedict's greatest miracle, for in this slim volume of about eighteen thousand words divided into sevnty-three terse chapters, Benedict set the course of Western monasticism. The *Rule* interweaves advice, admonishment, irony, and exhortation to great effect. It casts a warm eye on human frailties: "We read that monks should not drink wine at all, but since the monks of our day cannot be convinced of this, let us at least agree to drink moderately, and not to the point of excess" (*RB* 40). Yet it can be as strict as a one-room schoolmarm: "Permission to speak should seldom be granted even to mature disciples . . . speaking and teaching are the master's task; the disciple is to be silent and listen" (*RB* 6). Above all, the *Rule* aims to teach monk or nun how to grow closer to God and to a blessed life; Abbot Huerre suggested that Benedict's book might well be titled *The Art of Living.*

A MONK'S DAY

Every Benedictine monk or nun participates without fail in three daily occupations. These activities will become warp and woof of the daily fabric of our monastic retreat; they need to be examined in detail before we begin. In Latin, the trio has a lovely cadence that rolls lightly off the tongue: *oratio, labor, lectio divina.* In English, these translate into prayer, work, and sacred reading. Each occupation supports the rest; all are indispensable. Let us consider each in turn and then weigh their cumulative effect.

Oratio, *or Prayer*

At the twin monasteries in Petersham, the day begins at cockcrow as monks and nuns hasten to the chapel for a forty-minute blend of chanted psalmody, scriptural reading, and silent prayer, known as Lauds. Six more "Hours," as they are called—even though they may last but a few minutes—occur each day, in keeping with the prescription in Psalm 119:164, "Seven times a day I praise you." (Some monasteries add an eighth Hour, known as Vigils, to conform to Psalm 119:62, "At midnight I rise to praise you.") The entire cycle is called the "Divine Office" or—the term preferred by Benedict—the *opus Dei* ("work of God"). This cryptic phrase encompasses both the work of prayer undertaken by every monk or nun and God's work in the soul of everyone who prays. Of the importance of *opus Dei* and the appropriate comportment of those who take part in it, Benedict writes:

> We believe that the divine presence is everywhere. . . .
> But beyond the least doubt we should believe this
> to be especially true when we celebrate the divine
> office. . . . Let us consider, then, how we ought to
> behave in the presence of God and his angels, and
> let us stand to sing the psalms in such a way that
> our minds are in harmony with our voices. (*RB* 19)

Ideally, monks and nuns never "say" the Divine
Office; instead, they sing it, customarily in Gregorian
chant. According to Benedict, the chant unfolds before
all of creation "in the presence of God and the angels,"
as well as that of human beings and even animals. (I
once saw a centipede march drunkenly down the nave
as a group of four nuns, known as a *schola*, sang a lovely Latin *alleluia*. The centipede careened this way and
that, in an ecstasy worthy of any saint, before coming
to a dead stop in front of the altar, where, as far as I
know, it said its centipedal prayers.) Through the
Divine Office, monks and nuns open a conduit
between heaven and earth, singing prayers up to God
and singing God's love down to us. They sing for all
who cannot sing (including the little centipede), and
they sing, tradition has it, in tandem with those whose
song never ends, the angels and archangels whose
voices soar beyond our normal range of hearing.

The seven Hours sanctify the daily round. Each
phase of the cycle—daybreak, early morning, mid-
morning, high noon, afternoon, evening, and sundown—
finds its particular qualities reflected in the nature of
its corresponding Hour, from the prismatic beauty of
Lauds at daybreak to the intimacy of Compline as
night closes in. Why seven Hours? Why not two or
twenty-four? In part to satisfy the exclamation of the
psalmist in the Hebrew Bible, "Seven times a day I

praise you" (Ps 119:164). In part, too, because seven notes imply an octave (the eighth note repeating the first on a higher scale), a measure inherent in such fundamental structures as the musical scale, the periodic table of the elements, and the Ptolemaic model of the solar system. Benedict's arrangement thus adheres to cosmic law; the *opus Dei* reflects the basic form of God's creation.

The monastic community always assembles for the Hours; one very rarely sees a monk or nun chanting alone. Most houses spend a great deal of time in choir: at Petersham, the total averages about two-and-a-half hours a day, while other monasteries may double or even triple that figure. At first glance, these numbers may scare us off, suggesting that chant has no place in private retreat. Nothing could be further from the truth. Benedictine monks and nuns encourage everyone to chant the Divine Office whenever possible; it would be most unmonastic to claim such a glorious activity as one's private preserve. I have found, from my own experience, that the Divine Office can be easily tailored to suit a personal retreat, whether conducted alone or with others, without doing violence to its basic nature.

For our three-day retreat, I propose that we restrict ourselves to the three most evocative Hours: Lauds, Vespers, and Compline. We will use for our texts the same selection of psalms, canticles, and biblical passages sung in Benedictine monasteries throughout the world (abbreviated here and there to accommodate our needs). I propose, in addition, that we chant the Hours at the same times each day as do monks and nuns inhabiting our local time zone. Through this close adherence to universal monastic practice, we will enjoy one of the principal blessings conferred by the Divine Office: the knowledge that we join our voices to those of countless others, forming a chain of prayer running around the globe, linked tightly to the great chain of prayer extending back through time to Moses and before.

In addition to praying the Divine Office, each Benedictine monk or nun devotes a portion of his or her day to private prayer. Such prayer ranges from contemplation to vocal petitions to specific practices such as the Jesus Prayer. On our retreat, we will become acquainted with all of these methods; detailed information will be provided in later chapters. We will find, despite their varied forms, that all private prayers share a curious double action: they initiate a new inner order, described by St. Paul as the "new self" that will bring us to God; and, by bringing us to God, they invite him to reorder us into this "new self." Asking which comes first is pointless; each supports the other, and anyone who prays will soon know the taste of both.

Labor, or Work

Monks and nuns engage in all sorts of work. They boil jams, sew vestments, keep bees, "write" icons—all this in addition to the jobs that crop up whenever any group of people live together, such as cooking, sweeping, nursing, and the like; and all this on top of the many hours spent in the *opus Dei* and private prayer. As anyone who visits a monastery can testify, sometimes (not too often!) the bustle smacks more of the corporate office than the Divine Office. Most of this activity brings in money to keep the ship afloat, each monastery being responsible for its own upkeep. Some enterprises—weaving, silk-screening, printing, and the like—result in objects of great beauty that monks and nuns believe reflect or at least point toward the beauty of God. For this reason and others, craft flourishes at most Benedictine houses.

Manual labor regulates the daily life of each monk and nun as surely as does the Divine Office (as the Shakers have it, "hands to work, hearts to God"). Working with one's hands serves, too, as a splendid opportunity for putting into practice lessons absorbed beneath reading lamps in the monastic library. While bumbling through work, we may catch a glimpse of ourselves as we really are, not as we imagine ourselves to be. My youthful fantasies of being a master potter crumbled after just a few hours on the wheel as I saw my precious bowls (so perfect in my mind's eye) morph to blobs and globs. I keep one of these bowls on my desk even now, a clay mirror that never lies. Such self-knowledge forms the necessary back-drop for any real efforts toward self-sacrifice and surrender to God; for how can we enter "the kingdom of God within" without a roadmap of our inner terrain? Making such a sketch of our foibles and follies—and, to be sure, our occasional successes—is a principal reward of manual labor. We will make much use of it on our three-day retreat, trying out a number of different activities, sustaining them as long as they prove fruitful, and then turning to something new.

Lectio Divina, *or Sacred Reading*

During my years as a professional book reviewer, often I would find my desk groaning under the weight of the latest publishing crop, books piled in mounds, pinnacles, and teetering towers, books of every species under the sun, crime thrillers and logic studies, fishing manuals and poetry collections, ancient myths and post-modern philosophy, cookbooks with no kitchen in sight, coffee-table books that I would shield as best I could from the contents of my leaking coffee cup. My job obliged me to review up to thirty books a month; sometimes, I read so many words in a single day that when I closed my eyes I could see nothing but armies of letters marching across an endless page. I fell asleep once to the frightful fancy that my blanket and mattress had become a book jacket, and I was the dreaded reading material in between. But how could I read myself? This metaphysical puzzle would trap me for hours in that queasy half-awake, half-asleep state where tiny mental torments swell to elephantine size. (I am happy to report that at last I learned to relax into sleep by asking God, the master reviewer, to read *me* cover to cover.)

In self-defense, I soon became adept at the secret skill of every book critic, a talent that all possess but none whisper abroad: I learned to skim. Skimming is not skipping, nor is it skimping; skimming is sliding down the page lickety-split, gobbling up everything, but spitting most of it out as soon as the taste is registered, while the mind absorbs only those passages that, through some sixth sense peculiar to heavy readers, contain the real meat and potatoes. Skimming works—but not always. As I discovered, three kinds of reading matter resist all skimming. Two are novels and poems, where every word, every image, every sound counts. The third is scripture. Here, too, everything matters. But in addition, a new factor comes into play: in the inviolable words of scripture we may discover Truth itself.

While reading scripture, then—and I did have to read it occasionally, for I specialized in books on religion—

I learned to listen with the utmost attention, to ruminate on each word, sentence, paragraph, insofar as I was capable of such a trying feat. *Ruminate* seems to be the only word that fits, for just as a cow chews its cud, we need to chew the words of scripture, to extract all the meaning, veiled or revealed. This, according to the great Benedictine historian Jean Leclercq, is the characteristic monastic way of reading. No easy task! For scripture (and this goes for all sacred texts, for Qur'an and Pali Canon as well as Holy Bible) consists of overlapping layers of content, style, and intention. Scripture, I discovered, resembles more a complicated piece of high cuisine than a candy that melts in the mouth.

Although I didn't know it at the time, in mulling over scripture in my bumbling, amateurish way, I was on the road to discovering the third daily task of monks and nuns, which Benedict called *lectio divina,* usually translated as "sacred reading." A monk or nun is asked to read slowly, reflectively, meditating on each passage. Often the words enter into permanent memory, surfacing when needed during prayer. For the first millennium or so, Christian monks and nuns read aloud, with enough vigor that some medieval texts describe reading as an athletic activity. Like all good exercise, it brings ample rewards. As the monk reads, it is said, the scripture enters his heart; and God, who dwells in scripture, slips in as well.

Traditional monastic practice restricts *lectio divina* to biblical or patristic texts. However, I believe that we can remain faithful to the monastic tradition during our retreat while expanding our selection of texts to include any dignified reading that brings us closer to God. Certainly, the most secure choice remains the Bible. But let us embrace whatever will help. Who can say what word, what text, what author will escort someone into the holy of holies? In *Pilgrim at Tinker Creek*, Annie Dillard mentions a plethora of odd titles—my favorite is *The Gentle Art of Tramping*—that she devoured on retreat. The guidelines are simple: read, don't glance; pore over the text with a steady mind and a yielding heart; read as if your life depended on it, as indeed it does. In the next chapter, the choice of books appropriate for retreat is discussed in detail.

What then of the cumulative effect of *oratio, labor,* and *lectio divina*? Let us return for a moment to *oratio*: we sing the Divine Office with head, heart, and soul; swept up by the chant, we fly to God, finding during our ascent a unity of being that too often eludes us. Particulars aside, this description applies equally well to all other monastic activities, to private prayer, manual labor, and sacred reading. In one and all, we look to be whole; we look for God, in whom we find our wholeness. We look for balance, the balance that we find only when at rest in the hands of God. I believe that through a monastic retreat based on Benedictine principles and practices, we will find something of what we seek. The Benedictine way teaches us, as Abbot Huerre so memorably puts it, how "to live so that we are glad to be alive."[5] It seems to me that in these words we have a suitable goal for our retreat, and for our life as well.

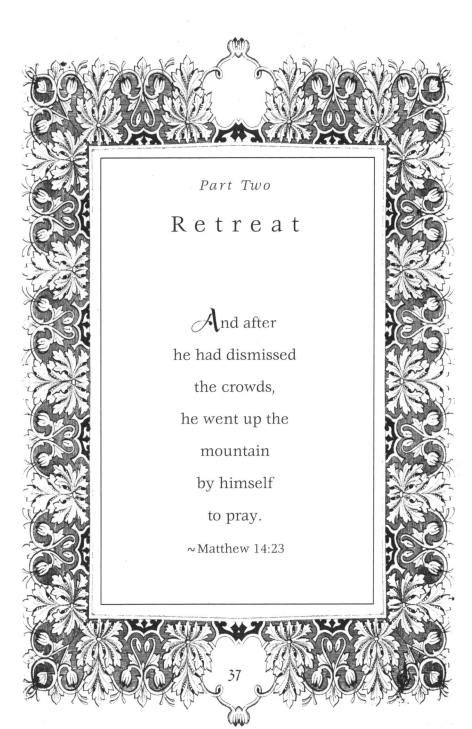

Part Two

Retreat

And after
he had dismissed
the crowds,
he went up the
mountain
by himself
to pray.

~ Matthew 14:23

37

𝒫REPARATIONS

One of my favorite mountain-climbing stories involves Maurice Wilson, an eccentric young Englishman who in the 1930s hatched the madcap scheme of scaling Mt. Everest solo by crashing a plane near the summit and hiking the rest of the way. There was something glorious in Wilson's mad caprice, for he pinned his hopes on faith in God, whom he believed would guide him safely to the peak, and on the extraordinary resilience of the human body, which he was convinced could withstand the brutal deprivation of oxygen, warmth, and food that an assault on Everest entailed. Wilson—who had never before flown a plane or climbed a mountain—was last seen trudging up Everest's north face at twenty-one thousand feet, carrying three loaves of bread, two cans of porridge, a British flag, and a camera. He didn't return, and his body was never recovered. Fifty years later, it's impossible to think of his exploit without admiring his pluck—how grand those old, solitary adventurers were!—and without wondering at his fool-hardiness. In Wilson's frozen fate lies an important lesson for our retreat: faith can carry you far, but planning counts as well.

Although the Bible describes many retreats, it offers few clues about preparation. Happily, we aren't abandoned to our own devices, for thousands of Christians have trekked before us into the spiritual hinterlands, and many of them have bequeathed helpful hints and cautions. One suggestion crops up so frequently that it might be called the Golden Rule of Retreat: *less is more.* The fewer encumbrances we lug along, the more time and space we make available for God. The classic cartoon of a Wall Street tycoon punching away at his calculator while sunbathing on the beach conveys a useful message: whether on vacation or retreat, it's best to leave the world and its demands behind. We have other work to do. Shopping lists, bits of office business, and "essential" phone calls amount to nothing but clutter. This excess baggage often sneaks in wearing a friendly mask, that of "spiritual" paraphernalia. Beware of too many books, too many meditations, too many ambitions. All these have their place, but on retreat they can be akin to the weights and chains that Jacob Marley's ghost dragged around as symbols of his avarice.

CHOOSING A TIME
AND A PLACE

The trophy for the strangest retreat site in history goes to St. Simeon Stylites (390–459), who endured twenty-three years atop a sixty-seven-foot-high pillar in the Egyptian desert. On this remarkable perch, only six feet wide, Simeon ate, slept, and prayed. He undertook this almost inconceivable feat of athletic asceticism in order to tame demons both inner and outer. No doubt great suffering was involved, although we may safely assume that Simeon had a head for heights and considerable tolerance for cramped living quarters. I don't encourage anyone to follow his example, although a faint echo of Simeon's experience may be heard in the ecstasies of Maurice Wilson and other mountaineers atop lofty peaks, as well as the strange, para-mystical trance that swept over astronaut Edward White during his pioneering 1965 space walk (a species of retreat that few of us may have the chance to enjoy), prompting him to refuse, for a few anxious moments, to return to his Gemini IV capsule.

Most of us will prefer a more mundane site for our time apart. Select with care! The locale we choose will become sacred territory, hallowed ground before the burning bush. Moses, John the Baptist, and a host of others chose the wilderness, where angels and demons roam, where heaven presses close to earth. Figuratively, at least, we must seek out our own wilderness for our retreat. For practical reasons, however, most of us will prefer to stay at home. This offers obvious advantages: Necessities lie close at hand, expenses are covered, and—of no small importance—security is assured. How, then, to approximate, in a familiar landscape of couches and electronic toys, some of the conditions of wilderness? Remember that we need silence and stillness. It's best, if possible, to arrange things so that you have the place to yourself; wait until the kids have been packed off to summer camp, until that noisy roommate takes her long-anticipated flight to the South Pacific. Keep the TV turned off, the phone unplugged. Arrange a specific hour for necessary phone calls from family or friends. If you cannot find solitude at home—or if you desire a retreat in monastic surroundings—take refuge in one of the hundreds of Benedictine or other Christian monasteries scattered throughout the world. Almost all monastic communities offer private rooms in exchange for a small donation, waived for those who can't afford to pay. As I indicated in chapter 2, the advantages of monastery retreats abound: silence, seclusion, the presence of senior monks or nuns who might be available for guidance, the chance to participate in Mass and the Divine Office, and, above all, the serene atmosphere that pervades these "school[s] for the Lord's service," as Benedict describes them (*RB*, prol.).

Whether house, hill, or monastic haven, our place of retreat needs to be outfitted in advance. Stock up on staples (food, toilet paper, batteries, and so on), to avoid unnecessary excursions to the local market. There is nothing more jarring, in the midst of a withdrawal from the world, than facing tabloid headlines in the check-out line. All important business should be settled before the retreat begins or after it ends; we must be able to immerse ourselves fully in the task at hand. Once, on a retreat with friends that lasted seven days, I volunteered to be the gofer, dashing out at all hours to fetch everything from frozen strawberries for the cook to a new ladder for the building team. At week's end, our house shone with new white walls, and the fruit pie sat benevolently in our stomachs, but the session had been for me largely a shambles, a disorienting succession of comings and goings in which zeal for business had trumped the needs of the heart.

CHOOSING THE RIGHT EQUIPMENT

No spiritual work takes place in a vacuum. Jesus made ample use of material supports: Torah scrolls for prayer; spit and mud to cure the blind; fish, wine, and bread to feed his flock and as signs of God's bounty. We too require materials; among the most important are the following:

A Chair or Cushion for Sitting

We will spend much of our time sitting: not lounging, lazing, cuddling, curling, snoozing, or slouching, but *sitting*, back straight, mind alert, heart awake in prayer. For prolonged prayer, it's best to hold the spine as erect as possible; doing so will assist with comfort, attention, and, according to certain schools of thought, the unimpeded flow of subtle energies throughout the body. This emphasis upon posture may surprise some people but, in truth, every aspect of the monastic way depends upon the body, since everything depends ultimately upon the Incarnation. "God became what we are that we might become what God is," as St. Irenaeus puts it. In the body we meet God; in the body God met us two thousand years ago in Palestine, and in the body of the Eucharist God meets us still today.

For sitting in prayer, many people prefer a hard, straight-backed chair. A meditation cushion will also do. The important thing is comfort so that we can remain still for a long stretch—at least twenty minutes—without pain or fidgeting.

Books

Books have voices as surely as do people: when we ask what books to bring on retreat, we ask which voices will break (and by breaking, perhaps deepen) the silence of our weekend. One of the most famous stories in the Bible recounts the retreat of Elijah in a cave on Mt. Horeb:

> And behold, the Lord passed by, and a great and strong wind rent the mountains, and broke in pieces the rocks before the Lord, but the Lord was not in the wind; and after the wind an earthquake, but the Lord was not in the earthquake; and after the earthquake a fire, but the Lord was not in the fire; and after the fire a still, small voice. (1 Kgs 19:11–12, RSV)

We, too, must let whirlwinds, earthquakes, and conflagrations pass by while seeking the "still, small voice" of God: a voice so gentle, so muted, that the clamor of ordinary life easily drowns it out. In order to hear this voice, we must silence the world; therefore, I suggest a prohibition on all literature that inflames the emotions or senses or that draws us back into our ordinary worries and obsessions. This includes not only reading related to our jobs, but also books that trade in sensationalism or gossip. Beach-chair best-sellers, newspapers, and magazines that cater to ephemeral interests are best left behind or placed out of sight.

What reading will help us in our search for God? I'm happy to say that the list is long, varied, and exciting:

Holy Bible. Both Judaism and Christianity hold the Bible to be the inspired word of God. While reciting the Divine Office, you will become familiar with many psalms and canticles. Don't limit your experience to these brief, if exquisite, excerpts. I urge you to open the Bible anywhere and read attentively; you will not fail to be rewarded.

The Rule of St. Benedict. I strongly recommend that you tote along a copy of the *Rule*, which can be picked up for a few dollars at most large bookstores. You can read the entire work—it's a marvel of brevity—or dip in at random. I suggest close study of chapters 4–7, in which Benedict lays the foundations of monastic practice through his discussions of obedience, silence, humility, and what he calls "tools for good works," seventy-one counsels beginning with the scriptural injunction to "love the Lord God with your whole heart, your whole soul, and all your strength" and ending with the impeccable advice to "never lose hope in God's mercy" (*RB* 4).

Prayer and poetry anthologies. The selection is vast. You might explore prayers by such saints as Augustine, Anselm, and Francis, or poems by such writers as Dante, John Donne, or George Herbert.

Monastic writings. Works by monks and nuns hold a special place on our three-day retreat. Recommended texts include:

✦ Anonymous, *The Cloud of Unknowing.* A terse, practical, immensely influential guide to contemplative prayer by a thirteenth-century Benedictine monk.

✦ St. Anselm of Canterbury, *Prayers and Meditations.* A great eleventh-century Benedictine theologian, philosopher, and bishop offers poetic reflections upon sin and salvation.

+ St. Athanasius, *Life of Antony*. The first and best biography of the prototypical monk, by a fourth-century monk, bishop, and doctor of the Church.

+ Abbot John Chapman, *Spiritual Letters*. A collection of letters on contemplative prayer by a twentieth-century abbot of Downside Abbey, England.

+ Dame Felicitas Corrigan, *A Benedictine Tapestry*. A delightful collection of essays on Benedictine life and mores by a nun of Stanbrook Abbey, England, whose life (1908–2003) spanned most of the twentieth century.

+ Abbot Hugh Gilbert, *Unfolding the Mystery*. Homilies and conferences on the mystery of Christ and his presence in the liturgy, by the current abbot of Pluscarden Abbey in Scotland.

+ St. Gregory the Great, *Life of St. Benedict*. The traditional biography of the great saint and founder of Western monasticism, by a sixth-century saint and pope.

+ Brother Lawrence of the Resurrection, *The Practice of the Presence of God*. Instructions on how to experience God's loving presence, by a Carmelite cook and cobbler.

+ Thomas Merton, *The Contemplative Life*. A well-known twentieth-century Cistercian monk explains the rudiments of monastic spirituality.

+ Edith Stein (St. Teresa Benedicta of the Cross), *The Science of the Cross*. A twentieth-century German-Jewish Carmelite nun and martyr explores the teachings of St. John of the Cross.

+ St. Teresa of Avila, *Life*. The brilliant autobiography of a great sixteenth-century Carmelite saint.

+ St. Thérèse of Lisieux, *The Story of a Soul*. The autobiography of a nineteenth-century Carmelite nun, a startling blend of adolescent angst and spiritual insight. Probably the most widely read Catholic text of the last 150 years.

Prayer Beads

In Istanbul's Grand Bazaar, that vast underground labyrinth of teahouses, kebab stands, and ramshackle shacks smelling of incense and yogurt, the grizzled old man sidled up to me, eyes aglitter. "You like my rugs," he said in thickly accented English, "the most beautiful rugs in the world." He was right; I had been furtively admiring a cream-and-rose prayer rug that had won my heart. Although I tried to be surreptitious—friends had warned me about the legendary rapacity of the bazaar hawkers—the old man zeroed in on the rug I coveted.

"Perfect weave," he said. "Worth much, very much." He then named an impossibly high price. I countered with a bargain-basement offer. We bickered back and forth, while sipping from copper cups of steaming sweet tea, a ubiquitous accompaniment to all wheeling and dealing in Turkey. Our palaver went nowhere, and finally the salesman threw up his hands, exclaimed "No sale, my friend," and handed me his business card for future use. I slipped it into my jacket.

In the process, my watchband snagged on something inside my pocket. I tugged, and out fell an Orthodox Christian prayer rope—a thick black circlet of cord braided into fifty knots, with a small cloth cross attached. I had bought the rope a few months earlier, in order to practice the Jesus Prayer (see chapter 5 for a description of this prayer). The salesman swooped down and snatched it up. "Ah, prayers!" he shouted. "You do prayers!" He then pulled from his own pocket a nearly identical rope and waggled it before my eyes. The only obvious difference was that the cross was replaced by a thick tuft of dangling threads. It was a *subha*, an Islamic knotted prayer strand. "I do prayers too," he said, beaming at me like a long-lost brother. He then gave me a deep look and said, "Now we can do business." Twenty minutes later, I walked out of the bazaar with my prayer rug bundled under my arm.

Thanks to this gruff Turkish shopkeeper, I had stumbled upon the noblest of secret societies: the universal union of prayer rope users. We tend to define religions by their differences, epitomized by their distinguishing signs: cross, Qur'an, bodhi-tree. But, as I have learned, the prayer rope binds together almost every faith on earth. In Tibet, Egypt, Ireland, Chile— wherever people pray (and where don't people pray?)—the prayer rope can be found. It serves first and foremost as a mnemonic aid to keep one's place in a complex sequence of worship. It also reminds the user of his or her commitment to the religious life. The cord's texture, silky or smooth, its comforting thickness when nestled in a pocket, the clack of the beads (most prayer ropes have beads of plastic, glass, bone, or seashell in place of knots; my wife owns a small one, known as a chaplet, beaded with compressed rose petals)—all this summons us to prayer. Finally, the small hand-held prayer rope symbolizes the great rope of prayer that binds us to all who pray and all who have prayed, in the world community of faith.

Christian prayer ropes come in two forms: as a rosary with beads or as a knotted cord. Western Christianity favors rosary beads, which made their appearance, tradition tells us, when St. Dominic received the first set from the Blessed Virgin Mary in 1214. Eastern Christianity prefers the cord, known by the generic term of "prayer rope." On the second day of our retreat, we will pray the Jesus Prayer. Although most people associate this practice with the Orthodox rope, rosary beads work just as well and will be much easier to obtain. Beads or rope may also, of course, be used to pray the Catholic rosary, a lovely and profound sequence of Hail Marys, Our Fathers, and other venerable prayers. I recommend obtaining a rosary or prayer rope before beginning the retreat; it will ground and elevate your prayer.

Miscellaneous Tools

Because of its doctrines of Creation and Incarnation, Christianity places great importance upon physical signs of God's presence: thus the significance of miracle stories—changing water into wine, restoring sight to the blind—throughout the New Testament and the long history of the Church. This emphasis also explains why Christians like to incorporate so many material objects—incense, flowers, water, icons, prayer cards, candles, weavings, statues, musical instruments, and more—into prayer and worship; everything in creation, made by God and reflecting to a greater or lesser degree the divine beauty, may serve as an offering to God or as a vehicle for contemplation. I urge you to explore this important aspect of the Christian sensibility. You might, for example, for the duration of your retreat (or longer), erect a prayer niche with a crucifix at the center, accompanied by a spring of winterberry or a few roses; nothing better focuses the mind, regulates the senses, and awakens the heart.

CHOOSING A SAINT

I'll never forget my first visit to Malta, that limestone chip in the blue-green Mediterranean, home of my maternal ancestors. One day my great-aunt Nena, a jolly woman well into her eighties, escorted my wife, my mother, and me to the chapel of Madonna Tal-Herba ("Madonna of the Ruins") in Birkirkara, a town just west of the capital city of Valletta. Here in a shadowy chapel basement hung scores of votive offerings: canes, walkers, artificial limbs, and crude illustrations in charcoal or oil (some of them executed by my grandfather, John) of shipwrecks, car crashes, volcanic eruptions, and other spectacular disasters. Each of these offerings, my great-aunt told us, commemorates a miracle. This battered crutch belonged to a girl healed of lameness; this painting depicts a sailor snatched from a shark's jaws. Invariably, the lucky survivor ascribed his escape to Madonna Tal-Herba—the local manifestation of the Blessed Virgin Mary—or to a beloved patron saint. Who would care to argue with men and women who have come within a hairsbreadth of death and thus have earned the right to speak their minds? In this dimly lit cellar, I saw demonstrated in all its grit and grandeur the ancient Christian practice of devotion to the saints.

From earliest times, Christians have turned to their holy predecessors for help. Some find it strange to pray to the dead, even the saintly dead. Yet the custom is found in almost every religion; it seems to be embedded in the psyche, encoded in the soul's DNA. The saints link heaven and earth, life and afterlife. By virtue of their exemplary lives, they sit with God. We pray to them, above all, in order to request their intercession with God, fountain of all gifts, on our behalf or on behalf of those for whom we pray. In time a saint may become a dear friend to whom one turns for advice, succor, and companionship. This solidarity between the living and the dead has been put most beautifully by St. Thérèse of Lisieux, who on her deathbed in 1896 (at the age of twenty-four) wrote, "I want to spend my heaven doing good on earth."

I urge you to pray to a saint throughout the retreat. Pray to him or her as a friend, an intimate, as someone who knows your sufferings, your hopes. Pray that he watch over you, protect you, and give you strength; pray that he light your way to God. Which saint, you may ask, will be right for me? A fair question; to paraphrase what Tolstoy said regarding families at the beginning of *Anna Karenina*, "Every saint is dissimilar in his own way." Every saint is radically himself. We call these men and women saints for just this reason: not because they have erased their personal identities by drinking a bland potion called "sanctity," but because in their surrender of self they have realized themselves to the utmost. There is no better expression of this idea than the unforgettable saying attributed to Rabbi Zusya: "When I die, God will not ask me, 'Why were you not Moses?' Surely He will ask me, 'Why were you not Zusya?'"

Below you will find a list of seven saints to whom you may wish to turn in devotion and prayer. The selection is not arbitrary—these saints are of particular interest to those on monastic retreat—but I might easily have chosen seven or seven thousand others, for all saints deserve and welcome our prayers. Don't feel bound to the names on this list. Perhaps the saintliest person in your experience is your deceased grandmother; then pray to and for her.

The Blessed Virgin Mary: Highest and most beloved of all saints, *Theotokos*, Mother of God.

St. Joseph: Husband of the Blessed Virgin Mary. A carpenter revered for his role as protector of the Holy Family. Patron saint of workers and travelers.

St. Benedict: Founder of Western monasticism. See chapter 2 for more information.

St. Scholastica: Twin sister of St. Benedict, the prototypical nun and protagonist in a celebrated Benedictine legend (which may be based on fact). During one of her rare visits with Benedict, Scholastica was dismayed when her brother rose early in the evening to return to his monastery. She prayed for a storm to detain him. Instantly lightning flashed, rain fell in torrents, and Benedict returned to his seat for a long conversation (and perhaps a benevolent scolding). In Benedictine tradition, Scholastica's prayer exemplifies the primacy of love over regulations.

St. Mary Magdalene: A close follower of Jesus and the first to see him after his resurrection. The prototype of the sinner turned saint; patron of all who mend their ways.

St. Thérèse of Lisieux: The most celebrated modern saint, author of the celebrated autobiography *The Story of a Soul*. A paragon of humility and simplicity, founder of the "Little Way." For more on St. Thérèse, see chapters 4 and 6.

Blessed Charles de Foucauld: A French aristocrat, explorer, and linguist who became a hermit in the Saharan desert, exemplifying the life of poverty, prayer, and love. Martyred by an Islamic jihadist in 1916, his life and writings, with their emphasis upon holiness and contemplation in daily life, have wielded an enormous influence upon modern Christian thought and practice.

SETTING AN AIM

Every so often I teach a college class in nature writing, a genre that demands, among other things, a knack for observing nature in the raw. A few weeks into the course, one issue arises without fail: how to prepare for our field trips. Everyone agrees on the necessary supplies: notebook, pencils, sunscreen, first aid kit, insect repellant, water bottles, and the like. Debate always breaks out, however, over one particular: whether we should read background material in order to get a sense of what to expect before plunging into the wilderness. Some students say no, insisting that this will prejudice us against new experience. We will see only what we expect to see, and the freshly-minted surprises of nature will escape our eyes. Others say yes: minds as well as rucksacks must be well-supplied, or we will lack the necessary compasses, both mental and material. To help settle the argument, I have the students read the following passage from Thoreau's "Seeing":

> Nature does not cast pearls before swine. There is just as much beauty visible to us in the landscape as we are prepared to appreciate—not a grain more. . . . The scarlet oak must, in a sense, be in your eye when you go forth. We cannot see anything until we are possessed with the idea of it. . . . I find that first the idea, or image, of a plant occupies my thoughts, although it may at first seem very foreign to this locality, and for some weeks or months I go thinking of it and expecting it unconsciously, and at length I surely see it, and it is henceforth an actual neighbor of mine. This is the history of my finding a score or more of rare plants which I could name.[1]

Thus speaks the master literary woodsman: without preparation, we will see nothing. To underscore this idea, I remind my students of the eating habits of the common frog. The frog cannot see a stationary insect; the idea of a non-moving food supply lies beyond the scope of its amphibian brain. If someday we meet an intelligent frog and explain to it that insects continue to exist while at rest, this knowledge will surely open up a vast new empire of food, a worldwide bug-restaurant of sorts, for that lucky frog. So it is with us. When someone blind from birth acquires sight, at first he sees the world as smears and blurs and blobs of color. Time must pass before that trembling brown rope topped with green becomes a maple tree, before that soft white ball six feet off the ground becomes a lover's face. We need to be prepared to meet our experience.

In just the same way, we need to clarify our aims before we go on retreat. Only by having a goal toward which we strive will our struggles acquire meaning, savor, substantial value. What are we looking for during this time apart? New resources to help us in our everyday life? But what does this mean, exactly? Do we hope to root out bad habits, to pray better, to surrender to God's love? Our goal may be to experience, for the first time, a sense of God's presence. No small aim, that! I urge you to ponder what you hope to find on this retreat; by examining your wishes now, you may give your retreat a welcome focus. But bear in mind: our will is to do the will of God, and God's will may confound our expectations. Be ready for surprise; prepare to be unprepared.

FINDING THE PATTERN
OF THE RETREAT

Snowflakes have patterns, as do symphonies, stories, and all beautiful things. So too should our retreat. Happily, a good, reliable, useful pattern lies close at hand. Most of us will conduct our retreat on the weekend (although any three successive days will do). Christian tradition perceives, in the symbolic meaning of Friday, Saturday, and Sunday, just the structure that we need, for these three days recapitulate in a minor key the three most sacred days in history: Good Friday, Holy Saturday, and Easter Sunday. We can do no better than to base our retreat upon this sacred model, for whatever our particular aim, we all share a desire to die to dead habits and dead-end dreams and to arise to a new life of vitality and hope. No one expresses this wish more eloquently than St. Paul:

> You have stripped off the old self with its practices and have clothed yourselves with the new self, which is being renewed in knowledge according to the image of its creator. . . . Clothe yourselves with compassion, kindness, humility, meekness, and patience. Bear with one another and, if anyone has a complaint against another, forgive each other; just as the Lord has forgiven you, so you also must forgive. Above all, clothe yourself with love, which binds everything together in perfect harmony. (Col 3:9–10, 12–14)

In Christian symbolism, Friday is the day of death, of letting go. On Friday we surrender to God's call of love and to our own wish for transformation through Christ. Saturday begins the process of renewal, a time of reflection, repentance, and *metanoia*. Sunday is the day of resurrection, on which we rejoice in our new-found life. This tri-fold template, sanctified by Christ's holy example, has inspired millions of men and women throughout the centuries. I believe that we make a wise choice by adopting it for our retreat.

The monastic practices that we will explore fit neatly into this tripartite pattern. Monks and nuns (and all Christians) engage in three basic types of prayer:

thanksgiving, petition, and adoration. In the first, we thank God for creating, sustaining, and blessing us; in the second, we ask God for assistance; in the third, we acknowledge, praise, and venerate God as ultimate mystery, source of being, the "I AM THAT I AM" of Exodus. All three modes of prayer will play a role in our retreat; we will emphasize one each day (while not forgetting the other two). The same pattern applies to the three monastic promises of stability, obedience, and *conversio*; we will emphasize stability on Friday, obedience on Saturday, and *conversio* on Sunday, while drawing sustenance from all each day.

To lend backbone to our efforts, each day we will undertake the Divine Office, manual labor, and *lectio divina*. Together, these constitute the axis of our retreat, around which all other events and actions revolve. We should make every effort to engage in these three essential activities as faithfully as possible. At the same time, bear in mind that we have withdrawn from ordinary life in search of prayer and perspective, not imprisonment. Decide for yourself when discipline becomes oppressive or laxness sloppiness. Too many "spiritual exercises" can be another way of stuffing the day with chores, to avoid the real work of renewal in Christ. At the same time, we all need a framework in which to grow, like the lattice that supports the climbing rose. There is nothing more discouraging upon retreat than to find yourself stuck in a corner, twiddling your thumbs. To avoid this, our retreat program distributes a number of activities throughout the day. None will suit everyone. All are optional.

The diagram opposite shows the overall pattern of the retreat.

Ᵽᴀᴛᴛᴇʀɴ ᴏꜰ ᴛʜᴇ Ꝛᴇᴛʀᴇᴀᴛ

DAY ONE

Theme: Detachment, death
Prayer: Thanksgiving
Prayer practice: Practice of the presence of God
Schedule: Morning contemplation
                     Lauds
                     Breakfast
                     Prayer, work, *lectio divina*
                     Lunch
                     Prayer, work, *lectio divina*
                     Vespers
                     Evening contemplation
                     Dinner
                     Recreation
                     Compline

DAY TWO

Theme: Gestation, Transformation
Prayer: Petition
Prayer practice: The Jesus Prayer
Schedule: Same as day one

DAY THREE

Theme: Resurrection
Prayer: Adoration and praise
Prayer practice: The Lord's Prayer
Schedule: Same as day one

THE NIGHT BEFORE

Many years ago, when my interest in Christian monasticism had just begun to bud, I signed up for a weekend retreat at St. Joseph's Abbey, a Cistercian monastery in central Massachusetts. The abbey's guest list fills up quickly, so I made my reservation nine months in advance. As the opening day of the retreat crept nearer, I began to fidget. This would be my first stay in a monastery, and I had no idea of what to expect. What if I didn't fit in? What if the monks turned out to be creepy? What if my wife and kids needed me at home? The worrier in me held center court.

By the time the great day arrived, I was a wreck. Driving up to the monastery gates, my stomach flip-flopped while a jackhammer pounded in my skull. I grabbed my bags, walked halfway up the flagstone path to the front door, then turned around and retreated to my car. There I was seized with disgust at my cowardice and turned back again. Halfway up, and again I reversed. I must have spun around five or six times; any monks watching from within might have thought me an eccentric Sufi, practicing his whirls in the Massachusetts snow. Finally, I steeled myself and knocked. A beaming man opened the door, his white robe dazzling against his coconut-brown skin. He ushered me in, and my life changed forever.

This comic episode drives home a simple truth: anxieties may be normal, but we cannot let them rule. We must banish all anticipation, all fear, all imagination about what we might encounter. The key is trust. Trust the retreat, trust the men and women who have refined these practices over the course of centuries. Trust God, who ceaselessly guards our welfare.

I would like to suggest that before going to sleep tonight you slip on a jacket and walk out under the stars. Those far-off furnaces began to blaze long before your birth, and they will continue to burn long after your death. The stars are emblems of eternity, semaphores of God. As their light spills down upon you, remember who you are. Remember who you wish to be. Remember why you are going on retreat. Remember the thousands who preceded you in this movement toward the desert and who will accompany you along the way: remember the saints and the apostles; remember Jesus Christ. Remember his love, which never ends.

Prayer

O Lord of Life, fountain of creation,
You breathe and the world begins.
You shape us from clay,
You hold us in your hands.
Guide us on this retreat
As we place ourselves wholly into your loving care.
Give us the wisdom, knowledge, and strength that we seek.
Give us what you will.

chapter 4

ᗪAY ONE

BEGINNING THE DAY

We start each day with twenty minutes of contemplative prayer, a silent sitting meditation during which we open ourselves to God. Contemplative prayer lies at the heart of monastic practice. In effect, it constitutes a retreat within our retreat, a withdrawal into the Holy of Holies, whose doors open only when we reach a state of profound recollection and receptivity. This practice requires no words, no implements, no ritual. In contemplative prayer we strip naked before God.

The Christian tradition abounds in great contemplatives, from St. John the Evangelist at the end of the first century to the Saharan hermit Blessed Charles de Foucauld during the twentieth. But the prototype of all contemplatives remains Mary, sister of Martha:

> Now as they went on their way, he [Jesus] entered
> a village; and a woman named Martha received
> him into her house. And she had a sister called
> Mary, who sat at the Lord's feet and listened to his
> teaching. But Martha was distracted with much
> serving; and she went to him and said, "Lord, do
> you not care that my sister has left me to serve
> alone? Tell her then to help me." But the Lord
> answered her, "Martha, Martha, you are anxious
> and troubled about many things; one thing is need-
> ful. Mary has chosen the good portion, which shall
> not be taken away from her." (Lk 10:38–42, RSV)

We too can begin our day by choosing the "good portion," the "one thing needful." In Mary's gesture, we see
the essential simplicity of contemplative prayer, for it
consists in nothing other than this: putting aside our
anxieties and troubles in order to sit at God's feet. A few
people may worry that contemplation is reserved for
spiritual adepts, a belief unfortunately promoted now
and then in the history of the Church. But as the gospel
passage above suggests, contemplation—like retreat—is
meant for all seekers after God, beginning or advanced.
You need have no fears on that account.

What takes place during contemplative prayer?
Some saints speak of divine energies, rays of darkness,
or infused graces entering the soul. Others liken the
process to illumination by God, the Sun of our spiritual
cosmos:

> For it is the God who said, "Let light shine out of
> darkness," who has shone in our hearts to give the
> light of the knowledge of the glory of God in the
> face of Jesus Christ. (2 Cor 4:6)

Perhaps the best definition comes from Gregory the
Great, who describes contemplation as "resting in
God." Our task is to await God, as humbly and simply

and quietly as possible, and to rest in his presence when and as he bestows it. Martha's bustle has no place here. We sit and we wait, hearts longing for God, minds distilled to a state of loving attention. We may hope for immediate results; we may even dream of attaining the highest stages of prayer, which the great Spanish Carmelite saints depict as a mystical marriage with God. But we cannot know, much less judge, the manner or means of God's work within us. Don't be discouraged if you see no evidence of change. God's activity is frequently invisible, unfolding at levels far below or above conscious thought, initiating a transformation whose results may become apparent far in the future, perhaps at—or after—the moment of death.

THE METHOD OF
CONTEMPLATIVE PRAYER

It's best to begin contemplation soon after arising for the day. Start by sitting in a comfortable position, arms relaxed, hands in lap. The spine should be erect. Imagine that a string has been attached to the top of your head and is gently pulling you upwards; this motion straightens and relaxes the spinal column. Not only will you find this position comfortable—it can be sustained for hours, if necessary, without undue strain— but it has symbolic importance as well, for only an erect posture befits our stature as children of God (we hear, in common speech, echoes of the symbolism of verticality in terms like *rectitude* and *moral uprightness*).

Once you have established a stable, upright position, sit quietly, without fidgeting. Take a few minutes to make sure that mind and body are tranquil, free from tension. Let your limbs relax, your breath grow soft, slow, and steady. During contemplation, says John of the Cross, Creator and creature breathe with the same breath. Breath anchors our prayer. If in the midst of your contemplation you suddenly discover yourself lost in fantasy, remembering yesterday's flirtation or anticipating tonight's dinner, don't be concerned. Simply return to your breathing. Let its rhythm steady you and transport you inward to begin again your silent vigil. To anchor your thoughts, it often helps to repeat silently a simple phrase of one or a few syllables, perhaps "Lord have mercy" or "Thy will be done," or simply, as the author of *The Cloud of Unknowing* advises, just "God" or "Love." Or you may wish to try a longer prayer and match it to your breathing. One possibility is the Jesus Prayer: "Lord Jesus Christ, have mercy on me, a sinner" (discussed more fully in chapter 5). Try saying the first part of the prayer on the in-breath and the second part on the out-breath, keeping your breathing soft and regular. Whatever words you choose, please don't worry too much about technique. An ancient saying reminds us that "if we take one step, God will take ten thousand." Our task is to take that first step, however clumsily, to cross the threshold into the inner chamber, there to await, with attention quickened by hope, the presence of God.

After twenty minutes, contemplation ends. We leave the prayer as gently as we can. The transition back to ordinary consciousness can be a time of fertile discovery: how can I retain the tranquility of body and mind that I discovered during the prayer? Learn the "taste" of this final moment of prayer, just before the world invades with all its pricks and prods.

FIRST ADVENTURES

Once we have finished our morning contemplation, we may want to explore our surroundings. We have pointed our soul's compass toward the true north of God; now it is time to orient ourselves in relation to the outer world. In a strange location, say a monastic guesthouse or an isolated cabin, we instinctively feel the need for such exploration. But I recommend it even if your retreat takes place at home; most people know much less about their habitations than they think!

Orientation can take many forms. For some aboriginal peoples, it entails locating the four cardinal directions. Huichol Indians on the sacred peyote hunt always begin in this way and recheck their position throughout the pilgrimage to know just where they stand in relation to their richly imagined cosmos, thick with ancestors, animals, and gods invisible to ordinary sight but revealed to the shaman and his disciples. Christianity, too, makes much of the cardinal directions; in Gothic cathedrals, for example, the main door faces west (toward the setting sun, land of the dead and the Last Judgment) while the altar faces east (toward the rising sun and Jerusalem, site of Christ's Resurrection).

Orientation involves more, however, than finding one's little place in the universe; it also means finding the universe in one's little place. During a retreat at a lovely Quaker farmstead in rural Massachusetts, I wound up in a cabin that had no electricity. As the sun fell on the first day, I realized that I would soon be left in pitch blackness, for I had neglected to pack a flashlight or candles (so much for careful planning). Sure enough, I cracked elbows and shins more times that evening than I care to remember. The next morning, I determined to befriend my environment; I spent the next several hours learning every stick of furniture, every sagging rafter, every cobwebbed window pane.

As the cabin and I became acquainted, I warmed toward my temporary home; this, I realized, was the space set aside for me on my mission to the interior of the heart. I began to love this little cabin and to see in its crude pine walls and blotchy floor the outlines of grace. For most of us, God does not speak in abstract reasoning but in the concrete friction and knocks of everyday life. In the rough boards of this cabin, in my stinging elbows and bruised knees, I began to sense God's presence, benevolent and amused. During my explorations, I found a spider: an orange and black little fellow living on a frayed web beneath the sink. This spider became my companion during these adventures. I never spoke to him, or he to me, but during my meditations I was often aware of his presence: silent, solitary, industrious in his own spidery way, on permanent retreat from the great pine forests outside our walls, a hermit of the animal world.

TODAY'S THEME:

DETACHMENT, OR DEATH

The theme for today is surrender, detachment, or—not to beat around the bush—death. But why speak of dying at the beginning of retreat? Haven't we sequestered ourselves in search of renewal, rebirth, the dawn of new possibilities? Yes, and for just that reason, death must play its part. To see why, let's consider the astonishing case of the blind Frenchman, Jacques Lusseyran.

Time: May 3, 1932. Place: a school room in Paris, France. The bell sounds for recess; in the ensuing commotion, a seven-year-old boy falls against a desk, smashing his spectacles, driving glass splinters into his right eye. The eye goes blind forever; a few days later, the other eye follows suit, through "sympathetic ophthalmia." A tragedy? Let us hear how Lusseyran himself evaluates the aftermath of this event that utterly changed his life: "Since the day I went blind I have never been unhappy."[1]

Incredible, preposterous. How can this be? Lusseyran admits that at first he reacted as we might expect, horrified at his involuntary and permanent retreat from the world of sight. He hated his blindness, despised his weakness, despaired over his future. Then one day, "and it was not long in coming," a truth dawned on him: "I realized that I was looking in the wrong way. . . . I was looking too far off, and too much on the surface of things."[2] Out of necessity, the little boy learned to see in a different way:

> I began to look . . . at a world closer to myself, looking from an inner place to one further within, instead of clinging to the movement of sight toward the world outside. Immediately the substance of the universe drew together, redefined, and peopled itself anew. I was aware of a radiance emanating from a place I knew nothing about, a place which might as well have been outside me as within. But radiance was there, or, to put it more precisely, light.[3]

In time, this revelation—no other word seems appropriate—carried Lusseyran into extraordinary adventures inner and outer. His senses burst into magnificent new life: He heard a Bach concerto as a cascade of colors; he handled an apple and "didn't even know whether I was touching it or it was touching me. As I became part of the apple, the apple became part of me. And that was how I came to understand the existence of things."[4]

Less than a decade later, Nazi tanks rolled over France. In response, Lusseyran founded—at the age of sixteen!—the Volunteers of Liberty, one of the most important of the French underground resistance groups. His ability to judge character had become so acute that he took on the critical job of screening all recruits. By discerning minute fluctuations in the human voice—the signal of moral rot—he could sniff out a traitor instantly. Just once he disregarded the promptings of his intuition. The error landed him in Buchenwald, where the blind boy became the light of the camp, as he explains:

> Light had become a substance within me. It broke into my cage, pushed by a force a thousand times stronger than I. . . . There was one thing left which I could do: not refuse God's help, the breath he was blowing upon me. . . . I could try to show other people how to go about holding on to life. I could turn toward them the flow of light and joy which had grown so abundant in me. From that time on they stopped stealing my bread or my soup. It never happened again. Often my comrades would wake me up in the night and take me to comfort someone, sometimes a long way off in another block.
>
> Almost everyone forgot I was a student. I became "the blind Frenchman." For many, I was just "the man who didn't die."[5]

How can we sum up this amazing story? Forced into exile from the world of sight, from all the visual cues and codes that we take for granted, Lusseyran discovered a new language of the heart. He learned "with absolute certainty that everything in the world was a sign of something else." "Some people would say I had faith," he writes, "and how should I not have it in the presence of the marvel which kept renewing itself?"[6]

I've recounted Jacques Lusseyran's story at length, because in it we see the spiritual meaning of death: death as shedding of old skin that binds us, the shucking of old habits that blind us, death as the prelude to spiritual rebirth. Said Jesus to Nicodemus, "Truly, truly, I say to you, unless one is born anew, he cannot see the kingdom of God" (Jn 3:3, RSV).

TODAY'S PROMISE: STABILITY

On this first day of retreat, as we plunge into the ocean of the spirit, we might suffer anxiety or fear at the immensity of our task. We do well to remember that we haven't been cast adrift. We anchor ourselves in God, and we move on his abiding currents. Benedictines drop anchor by making a vow of stability, pledging themselves, for life, to the monastery where they received their spiritual formation. Through stability of place, the monk or nun seeks stability of heart— an ever more profound love of Jesus, accompanied by the courage to persevere on the monastic path.

These ambitions demand energy, sometimes great amounts of it. Although people take stability to imply standing still or even lassitude, nothing is further from the truth. When not immersed in contemplative prayer or stationed in the choir for Mass or the Divine Office, monks and nuns pitch into their work with a gusto that puts the ant and bee to shame. In a sense, this ceaseless striving rules the inner life as well, at least among many of the monks and nuns whom I have met; thus

Benedict in his *Rule* speaks of "hastening on to the perfection of monastic life" (*RB* 73). We perceive this
dynamic activity in the life of Jacques Lusseyran as
well. Once he discovered inner light, Lusseyran never
idled; to do so would have been to blind himself again,
this time willingly. Instead, he pressed onward, mold-
ing his inward vision into a beacon for others as well as
himself. Jacques Lusseyran and the Benedictines have
this also in common: underneath the furious enterprise
lies a center of absolute stillness, the eye of the hurricane, where they rest in the presence of God. In this
silent cathedral within the heart, all may find true stability, a home forever. Throughout this day, in all the
activities detailed below, we will ponder the meaning of
stability in our own lives.

THE DIVINE OFFICE

Legend has it that Immanuel Kant kept so strict a daily
routine that the housewives of Konigsberg set their clocks
by his morning constitutional. But we mustn't confuse
regularity with lack of inspiration; Kant gave the world a
philosophical system of dazzling originality and force. So
it is in the monastery as well. The regular round of private and communal prayer, sacred reading, and manual
labor, renewed every day of the year, across the decades,
down the centuries, has become the heartbeat of monasticism, the rhythmic expression of its vital life, a foundation of physical and mental discipline that gives rise to
true freedom of the spirit. The Divine Office stands at the
center of this firm discipline, this inspired life. The Office
comes first; when the bell sounds the Hour, monk or nun
hastens to the chapel (unless hospitality or other need
dictates an exception). Here the entire community offers

itself through prayer to God and to the world. Through our own efforts at the *opus Dei*, however tentative, feeble, or fumbling, we too share in this great endeavor and enjoy some measure of the stability that it brings.

For the sake of simplicity and serenity, we will cut back on the daily chant regimen, retaining three major Hours:

Lauds, or Morning Office (prayed before breakfast)
Vespers, or Evening Office (prayed before dinner)
Compline, or Night Office (prayed before retiring)

In the choice of texts for the Divine Office, we adhere strictly to custom. The selections for Friday, the first day of our retreat, are the same as those chanted on a typical Friday in Benedictine monasteries throughout much of the English-speaking world. The same goes for Saturday and Sunday.

The Hours retain the same structure each day, a great aid in the quest for stability. Here is the standard template:

· *L* · A · U · D · S ·

(MORNING OFFICE)

Introductory Prayer
Morning Psalm
Hymn
Psalm of Praise
Scripture Reading
Silent Prayer
Canticle of Zechariah
The Lord's Prayer
Concluding Prayer
Blessing

· V · E · S · P · E · R · S ·

(EVENING OFFICE)

Introductory Prayer

Psalm

Psalm

Hymn

Scripture Reading

Silent Prayer

Canticle of Mary

The Lord's Prayer

Concluding Prayer

Blessing

· C · O · M · P · L · I · N · E ·

(NIGHT OFFICE)

Introductory Prayer

Examination of Conscience

Psalm

Scripture Reading

Silent Prayer

Canticle of Simeon

Concluding Prayer

Blessing

Salve Regina

Before we begin the *opus Dei*, we must address an important question: how do we recite the psalms, canticles, readings, and prayers that constitute each Hour? Benedict offers a modicum of advice, telling us that the

Hours should be prayed "with humility, seriousness, and reverence" (*RB* 47). Each of these qualifiers carries its own cargo of meaning. "Seriousness" suggests that we recite the text while holding in mind its sacred character; "reverence" that we do so while remaining alert to the presence of God, who hears our every syllable and silence; "humility," that we do so while remembering our smallness and God's greatness. Needless to say, we can hardly keep these ideas in mind at all times; to try would guarantee distraction (like thinking about the location of letters on a keyboard while trying to type). Something else is needed, some ingredient that will bring along with it the requisite humility, gravity, and reverence.

In Christian monasticism, this element is found in the disposition, or inner posture, of the monk or nun in prayer. We may describe it as "relaxed attention" or "active passivity." We need to step aside and let the prayer pass unimpeded from our heart to God and back again. As for how to attain this state of spiritual transparency, perhaps the simplest suggestion is to say the Hour with grace. That word packs a multitude of meanings, some of enormous theological complexity. Keep it simple; picture a ballerina en pointe, a priest elevating the Host, a bride approaching the altar. In the bearing of each, you can catch a glimpse of what I mean, in this instance, by grace: delicate solemnity, spirited gravity, effortless effort.

My youngest son Andy often breaks into song when he dives into a beloved hobby, such as rearranging his collection of rocks and minerals. Singing expresses joy, at least for angels, birds, and children—and for monks and nuns singing the Hours. Nonetheless, many of us will shy away from singing the Divine Office, no

matter how blissful we feel. This is as it should be, for
to be attempted with any chance of success, Gregorian
chant demands considerable vocal training and a specialized knowledge of medieval neumes. Instead of
embarrassing ourselves and the great tradition in
which we participate, I suggest that we recite each
Hour aloud, quietly but firmly. Let me repeat: aloud.
This is essential. Vocalization gives to us—and summons from us—resources unknown in silent reading.
We absorb the exquisite beauty of psalm and canticle,
and we pour out this beauty upon the world. By sound-
ing the words, we take a stand: we declare ourselves to
God with our bodies as well as our minds.

Most of us will undertake this retreat alone, thus
missing the experience of the communal Divine
Office. Yet solitude holds certain advantages. Nietzsche
observed that "when we talk in company we lose our
unique tone of voice." On retreat, we talk by ourselves;
or rather, we engage in a private dialogue with God. As
a result, the "unique tone of voice" of each of us has a
chance to sound forth. This requires care. The words of
the Office should be enunciated as attentively as possible, with the voice originating in the chest rather than
the larynx; this will ensure the vocal resonance worthy
of sacred texts.

Posture plays its part in the Divine Office as well.
The words can be recited sitting or standing; either
way, as with contemplative prayer, an erect spine
helps. Try to keep fidgeting to a minimum; bear in mind
that we offer to God not only our voices but our entire
bodies. Recapture, if you can, the sense of profound recollection that you experienced during the depths of
contemplation. If this is unattainable, just do your best.
I've said the Divine Office in distress, in high dudgeon,

while dizzy with joy, and I've found that none of this matters much. Only prayer matters. If we empty ourselves of extraneous business, we will be filled only with prayer, and with the divine love that courses through prayer, and all will be well in the praying.

You may stand or sit through most of the Divine Office, but one other position comes into play now and then. To the conclusion of every psalm or canticle, monastic tradition appends a hymn of praise to God, known as the doxology:

> Glory be to the Father and to the Son and to the Holy Spirit, as it was in the beginning, is now, and ever shall be, world without end, Amen.

In this set phrase, we acknowledge God's glory (Greek *doxa*, Hebrew *kabod*), which both the ancient Hebrews and the early Christians understood as a radiant royal presence, and we bear witness to the Trinitarian doctrine of God as three persons in one, a self-reflective community of love. While reciting the doxology, it is customary in many monasteries to bow deeply from the waist. We find this beautiful gesture everywhere—Zen pupils bow to their *roshi*, knights to their ladies, peacocks to their peahens—enclosing in its simple form a wealth of meanings, including obeisance, humility, service, and gratitude. The bow has become my favorite moment during the Divine Office, and I believe that you will come to relish it as well.

One note of caution as we start the *opus Dei*: some of the passages may startle you with their ferocity. Remember that these psalms and canticles emerged in a world far removed from our own. War, plague, and famine ruled the day, and death knocked nightly at the door. God became, as the psalmist says, "our refuge and our strength." While conditions have changed—

although perhaps not so much as we may like—the power and value of this venerable tradition remains intact. Recite the scriptures with attention, and you will surely encounter, as did the ancient Israelites, the glory and tenderness of God.

THE DIVINE OFFICE FOR FRIDAY

·*L*·A·U·D·S·

(MORNING OFFICE)

INTRODUCTORY PRAYER

Lord, Open my lips, and my mouth will proclaim your praise.

(*Bow*) Glory be to the Father, and to the Son, and to the Holy Spirit. As it was in the beginning, is now, and ever shall be, world without end, Amen.

MORNING PSALM (PS 119:145-149)

With my whole heart I cry; answer me, O Lord.
    I will keep your statutes.
I cry to you; save me,
    that I may observe your decrees.
I rise before dawn and cry for help;
    I put my hope in your words.
My eyes are awake before each watch of the night,
    that I may meditate on your promise.
In your steadfast love hear my voice;
    O Lord, in your justice preserve my life.

(*Bow*) Glory be to the Father, and to the Son, and to the Holy Spirit. As it was in the beginning, is now, and ever shall be, world without end, Amen.

HYMN (IS 45:15–20)

Truly, you are a God who hides himself,
O God of Israel, the Savior.
All of them are put to shame and confounded,
the makers of idols go in confusion together.
But Israel is saved by the Lord
with everlasting salvation;
you shall not be put to shame or confounded
to all eternity.
For thus says the Lord,
who created the heavens
(he is God!),
who formed the earth and made it
(he established it;
he did not create it a chaos,
he formed it to be inhabited!)
I am the Lord, and there is no other.
I did not speak in secret,
in a land of darkness;
I did not say to the offspring of Jacob,
"Seek me in chaos."
I the Lord speak the truth,
I declare what is right.

(*Bow*) Glory be to the Father, and to the Son, and to the Holy Spirit. As it was in the beginning, is now, and ever shall be, world without end, Amen.

PSALM OF PRAISE (PS 100)

Make a joyful noise to the Lord, all the earth.
>   Worship the Lord with gladness;
>   come into his presence with singing.

Know that the Lord is God.
>   It is he that made us, and we are his;
>   we are his people, and the sheep of his pasture.
Enter his gates with thanksgiving,
>   and his courts with praise.
>   Give thanks to him, bless his name.
For the Lord is good;
>   his steadfast love endures forever,
>   and his faithfulness to all generations.

(*Bow*) Glory be to the Father, and to the Son, and to the Holy Spirit. As it was in the beginning, is now, and ever shall be, world without end, Amen.

SCRIPTURE READING (EPH 4:29-32)

Let no evil come out of your mouths, but only what is useful for building up, as there is need, so that your words may give grace to those who hear. And do not grieve the Holy Spirit of God, with which you were marked with a seal for the day of redemption. Put away from you all bitterness and wrath and wrangling and slander, together with all malice, and be kind to one another, tenderhearted, forgiving one another, as God in Christ has forgiven you.

SILENT PRAYER

(For a few minutes, we pray to God in silence and stillness. Our prayer may take whatever form suits the moment: thanksgiving, petition, praise, or adoration.)

CANTICLE OF ZECHARIAH (LK 1:68–79)

Blessed be the Lord God of Israel,
    for he has looked favorably on his people and redeemed
        them.
He has raised up a mighty savior for us
    in the house of his servant David,
as he spoke through the mouth of his holy prophets from of old,
    that we would be saved from our enemies and from the
        hand of all who hate us.
Thus he has shown the mercy promised to our ancestors,
    and has remembered his holy covenant,
the oath that he swore to our ancestor Abraham,
    to grant us that we, being rescued from the hands of our
        enemies,
might serve him without fear, in holiness and righteousness
        before him all our days.
And you, child, will be called the prophet of the Most High;
    for you will go before the Lord to prepare his ways,
to give knowledge of salvation to his people
    by the forgiveness of their sins.
By the tender mercy of our God,
    the dawn from on high will break upon us,
to give light to those who sit in darkness and in the shadow of
        death,
    to guide our feet into the way of peace.

(*Bow*) Glory be to the Father, and to the Son, and to the Holy
Spirit. As it was in the beginning, is now, and ever shall be,
world without end, Amen.

THE LORD'S PRAYER

Our Father, who art in heaven,
    hallowed be thy name.
Thy kingdom come, thy will be done,

On earth as it is in heaven.
Give us this day our daily bread,
    and forgive us our trespasses,
    as we forgive those who trespass against us.
And lead us not into temptation,
    but deliver us from evil.

CONCLUDING PRAYER

We ask this through Jesus Christ, your Son, who lives and reigns with you and the Holy Spirit, one God forever and ever, Amen.

BLESSING

May the Lord God bless us, guide us, guard us from evil, and bring us to life eternal, Amen.

· V · E · S · P · E · R · S ·

(EVENING OFFICE)

INTRODUCTORY PRAYER

God, come to my assistance; Lord, make haste to help me.

(*Bow*) Glory be to the Father, and to the Son, and to the Holy Spirit. As it was in the beginning, is now, and ever shall be, world without end, Amen.

PSALM (PS 116:1-9)

I love the Lord, because he has heard
    my voice and my supplications.
Because he inclined his ear to me,
    therefore I will call on him as long as I live.
The snares of death encompassed me;
    the pangs of Sheol laid hold on me;

I suffered distress and anguish.
Then I called on the name of the Lord:
>"O Lord, I pray, save my life!"

Gracious is the Lord, and righteous;
>our God is merciful.
The Lord protects the simple;
>when I was brought low, he saved me.
Return, O my soul, to your rest,
>for the Lord has dealt bountifully with you.

(*Bow*) Glory be to the Father, and to the Son, and to the Holy Spirit. As it was in the beginning, is now, and ever shall be, world without end, Amen.

PSALM (PS 121)

I lift up my eyes to the hills—
>from where will my help come?
My help comes from the Lord,
>who made heaven and earth.
He will not let your foot be moved;
>he who keeps you will not slumber.
He who keeps Israel
>will neither slumber nor sleep.

The Lord is your keeper;
>the Lord is your shade at your right hand.
The sun shall not strike you by day,
>nor the moon by night.

The Lord will keep you from all evil;
>he will keep your life.
The Lord will keep
>your going out and your coming in
>from this time on and forevermore.

(*Bow*) Glory be to the Father, and to the Son, and to the Holy Spirit. As it was in the beginning, is now, and ever shall be, world without end, Amen.

HYMN (RV 15:3–4)

Great and amazing are your deeds,
    Lord God the Almighty!
Just and true are your ways,
    King of the nations!
Lord, who will not fear
    and glorify your name?
For you alone are holy.
      All nations will come
      and worship before you,
for your judgments have been revealed.

(*Bow*) Glory be to the Father, and to the Son, and to the Holy Spirit. As it was in the beginning, is now, and ever shall be, world without end, Amen.

SCRIPTURE READING (JAS 1:2–4)

My brothers and sisters, whenever you face trials of any kind, consider it nothing but joy, because you know that the testing of your faith produces endurance; and let endurance have its full effect, so that you may be mature and complete, lacking in nothing.

SILENT PRAYER

(For a few minutes, we pray to God in silence and stillness. Our prayer may take whatever form suits the moment: thanksgiving, petition, praise, or adoration.)

CANTICLE OF MARY (LK 1:46–55)

My soul magnifies the Lord,
    and my spirit rejoices in God my Savior,
for he has looked with favor on the lowliness of his servant.
    Surely, from now on all generations will call me blessed;
for the Mighty One has done great things for me,

and holy is his name.
His mercy is for those who fear him
 from generation to generation.
He has shown strength with his arm;
 he has scattered the proud in the thoughts of their hearts.
He has brought down the powerful from their thrones,
 and lifted up the lowly;
he has filled the hungry with good things,
 and sent the rich away empty.
He has helped his servant Israel,
 in remembrance of his mercy,
according to the promise he made to our ancestors,
 to Abraham and to his descendants forever.

(*Bow*) Glory be to the Father, and to the Son, and to the Holy Spirit. As it was in the beginning, is now, and ever shall be, world without end, Amen.

THE LORD'S PRAYER

Our Father, who art in heaven,
 hallowed be thy name.
Thy kingdom come, thy will be done,
 On earth as it is in heaven.
Give us this day our daily bread,
 and forgive us our trespasses,
 as we forgive those who trespass against us.
And lead us not into temptation,
 but deliver us from evil.

CONCLUDING PRAYER

We ask this through Jesus Christ, your Son, who lives and reigns with you and the Holy Spirit, one God forever and ever, Amen.

BLESSING

May the Lord God bless us, guide us, guard us from evil, and bring us to life eternal, Amen.

· ☾ · O · M · P · L · I · N · E ·

(NIGHT OFFICE)

INTRODUCTORY PRAYER

God, come to my assistance; Lord, make haste to help me.

(*Bow*) Glory be to the Father, and to the Son, and to the Holy Spirit. As it was in the beginning, is now, and ever shall be, world without end, Amen.

EXAMINATION OF CONSCIENCE

(For a few moments, we think back over the day, paying particular attention to any failures in behavior toward ourselves or others. Do we see anything that troubles us in thought or deed? We resolve, simply and gently, to do our best tomorrow.)

PSALM (PS 86:1-7)

Incline your ear, O Lord, and answer me,
    for I am poor and needy.
Preserve my life, for I am devoted to you;
    save your servant who trusts in you.
You are my God; be gracious to me, O Lord.
    for to you do I cry all day long.
Gladden the soul of your servant,
    for to you, O Lord, I lift up my soul.
For you, O Lord, are good and forgiving,
    abounding in steadfast love to all who call on you.
Give ear, O Lord, to my prayer;
    listen to my cry of supplication.
In the day of my trouble I call on you,
    for you will answer me.

(*Bow*) Glory be to the Father, and to the Son, and to the Holy Spirit. As it was in the beginning, is now, and ever shall be, world without end, Amen.

SCRIPTURE READING (1 COR 13:1-7)

If I speak in the tongues of mortals and of angels, but do not have love, I am a noisy gong or a clanging cymbal. And if I have prophetic powers, and understand all mysteries and all knowledge, and if I have all faith, so as to remove mountains, but do not have love, I am nothing. If I give away all my possessions, and if I hand over my body so that I may boast, but do not have love, I gain nothing.

Love is patient; love is kind; love is not envious or boastful or arrogant or rude. It does not insist on its own way; it is not irritable or resentful; it does not rejoice in wrongdoing, but rejoices in the truth. It bears all things, believes all things, hopes all things, endures all things.

SILENT PRAYER

(For a few minutes, we pray to God in silence and stillness. Our prayer may take whatever form suits the moment: thanksgiving, petition, praise, or adoration.)

CANTICLE OF SIMEON (LK 2:29-32)

Master, now you are dismissing your servant in peace,
    according to your word;
for my eyes have seen your salvation,
    which you have prepared in the presence of all peoples,
a light for revelation to the Gentiles
    and for glory to your people Israel.

(*Bow*) Glory be to the Father, and to the Son, and to the Holy Spirit. As it was in the beginning, is now, and ever shall be, world without end, Amen.

CONCLUDING PRAYER

We pray you Lord, let your holy angels watch over us and let your love be with us always, through Christ our Lord, Amen.

BLESSING

May God grant us a peaceful night, a peaceful death, and perfect peace hereafter.

SALVE REGINA
(A PRAYER TO THE BLESSED VIRGIN MARY)

Hail holy Queen, mother of mercy,
    our life, our sweetness, and our hope.
To you do we cry,
    poor banished children of Eve.
To you do we send up our sighs,
    mourning and weeping in this valley of tears.
Turn then, o most gracious advocate,
    your merciful eyes toward us.
And after this, our exile,
    show to us the blessed fruit of your womb, Jesus.
O clement, o loving, o sweet Virgin Mary.

(The Great Silence descends, not to be broken until the next morning).

SACRED READING
FOR TODAY

I once knew a woman who bought all her clothes through mail-order catalogues. She adored shopping, and every week a new set of packages tumbled across her doorstep. Whenever I stopped by for a visit, I found her sofa and easy chairs festooned with dresses, blouses, skirts, and sweaters, tags intact. A few other items always lay close at hand: tape, cord, packing boxes, and stamps. For my friend had a little secret: she knew ahead of time that few of the clothes would fit (her postage bills must have been enormous). The source of her clairvoyance? Simple: she never ordered to match her current size, but to conform to an ideal shape, the slim self she had once been and planned to be again.

As with clothes, so with prayer. There's no point in struggling with sacred texts that just don't fit. It's not that we should settle for polyester; merely that different words suit different people. Bear this in mind when selecting the reading material for *lectio divina*. For each day of our retreat, I'll suggest one passage drawn from the New Testament and based on the theme of the day (I won't analyze the text for you, for *lectio divina* is another way that God speaks to each of us alone). Please don't feel bound by my selection. Whatever reading brings you closer to God is authentic *lectio divina*. Rather than pore over snippets of scripture, you might want to study an entire gospel or epistle during the span of the retreat. Nor should you feel compelled to read at a specific time; God awaits you always. Whatever and whenever you read, be sure to proceed slowly, masticating each sentence (as medieval monks would say) in order to extract its full nutrition. Today's suggestion for *lectio divina* is the parable of the sower: Matthew 13:1–23, Mark 4:1–25, or Luke 8:4–18.

MANUAL LABOR
FOR TODAY

Henry Thoreau's activities at Walden Pond suggest— but by no means exhaust—the range of manual work suitable for retreat: he erected a cabin, planted trees, cultivated beans, jawed with neighbors, measured snowdrifts, plumbed the pond, and hiked more often than his legend allows to the center of Concord. The same options apply to our time alone. Some of us may work at a craft, perhaps cooking, sewing, or weaving. Others may prefer sweatier tasks: hoeing a garden, uprooting weeds, repainting a shed. All these fit perfectly with retreat, for they keep hands occupied while the mind rests in God. If nothing else appeals, get on your knees and scrub the decks. From Jerusalem to Japan, dirt symbolizes confusion, obscuration, wandering off the path, while cleanliness signifies truth—and the ability to perceive it. As the Psalter reminds us, "Who shall ascend the hill of the Lord? And who shall stand in his holy place? Those who have clean hands and pure heart" (Ps 24:3).

However you choose to employ your hands, whether hammering a nail, weaving a tapestry, or washing a wall, remember that your task serves two ends. One is material and self-evident: by hammering the nail, you build the house. The second is spiritual and elusive: by hammering that nail, you build an inner house as well. To drive a nail is no mean accomplishment, but to drive a nail while in a state of prayer elevates you to another plane entirely. "Well then," you might ask, "How do I do this? I've cursed while hammering, but never yet prayed." But there's nothing mysterious about work-in-prayer. The key consists in expanding one's attention, lending part of it to God while the rest occupies itself with the task at hand. We do something akin whenever we talk while driving, or sing while bathing, or eat a hotdog while watching a ballgame. Notice that of these paired actions, one is predominantly physical, the other predominantly mental.

Tackling two mental tasks at once—say, counting forward and backward at the same time—is bound to short-circuit. For just this reason, our labor on retreat should be manual, leaving our minds free to turn to God. Joining sweat and prayer, we sanctify our activities; we become not only apprentice carpenters or potters or cooks, but—this may sound ambitious but it's no more than the bald truth—apprentice saints as well.

For this reason alone, we should learn to rejoice in our mistakes. We haven't set out to win the blue ribbon at the local 4-H but to win a truer way of life. I remember an incident during a group retreat many years ago. Five or six of us decided to paint the interior of a house. One young man, whom I will call "Sam"—a scholar more accustomed to scraping meaning from ancient parchment than old paint from walls—volunteered to prep and paint the staircase. For hours he scratched away at the flaking paint, stirring up clouds of plaster dust in the process. Soon a greasy film coated every surface in sight, including Sam, his coworkers, and the stairs. Finally Sam pronounced his prep work done and dashed upstairs to grab the paint. As he came back down, a five-gallon can of white latex in hand, he slipped on the dust. I shall never forget the look on his face—a mix of bewilderment, horror, and awe—nor the graceful arc made by the paint as it poured through the air, like a white ocean wave, before splashing across walls, banister, risers, floor, and the heads of the assembled painting team. It took us most of the day to clean up the mess.

From one perspective, Sam's tumble amounted to a perfect fiasco. But later he confided in me—and he meant it—that spilling the paint was "one of the best things that had ever happened" to him. Why? In part,

Sam said, because he prided himself on being a meticulous, mistake-free worker, and when the accident took place, he saw his inattention and vanity literally broadcast across the room. "Every time I climb those stairs," he said, "I'll remember who I really am." In part, too, he traced his good feelings to the clean-up, in which everyone took part, a concrete expression of the solidarity that can develop on a shared retreat. And then again, he added, there was a third reason, perhaps the best: we looked hilarious with white paint streaming down our faces. No doubt we did; Sam's mistake deflated a bit of our own self-importance as well.

TODAY'S PRAYER PRACTICE: PRACTICING THE PRESENCE OF GOD

In Andrew Davis's 1992 action film, *Under Siege,* Steven Seagal plays a cook on the *U.S.S. Missouri,* a warship slated for mothballs. When terrorists board the vessel to hijack a brace of nuclear-tipped missiles, the viewer soon discovers that beneath his chef's hat, Seagal wears (figuratively speaking) the black cap of a special Navy operative. Almost single-handedly, our hero routs the enemy and saves the West from nuclear holocaust. In this live-action cartoon, we can discern one of the oldest folklore motifs, that of the king in disguise. The theme crops up in one fairy tale after another: this frog is really a handsome prince; that tree, a sinuous dryad. Another variation involves the veiled master, the man or woman of impeccable attainments but unprepossessing—if not downright repellent— mien (George Lucas adopted this motif in the *Star Wars* trilogy for the character of Yoda, the fussy, frog-like,

900-year-old Jedi knight, as did Carlos Castaneda for his irascible Yaqui sorcerer, Don Juan).

As unlikely as it sounds, in the religious sphere such stories sometimes turn out to be true. The most unprepossessing figure may turn out to be a genius of sanctity. Consider Thérèse of Lisieux, that giddy teenager cloistered in an out-of-the-way Carmelite monastery, who became the most cherished saint of modern times, or Jean Vianney, the Curé d'Ars, whose advice in the confessional, dispensed from his tiny parish in an insignificant French village, brought solace to millions. One of the most striking examples of hidden sanctity comes to us from seventeenth-century Paris in the person of Brother Lawrence of the Resurrection. A self-described "clumsy lummox who broke everything," Brother Lawrence passed his entire adult life in monastic enclosure as a cook and cobbler. He never wrote a book, assembled a circle of pupils, or attained high office. He died as he lived, in utter obscurity. Yet a handful of his letters and other writings survived, and from them his followers culled an extraordinary spiritual method known as "the practice of the presence of God."

The heart of Brother Lawrence's method is this: we find God in the ordinary things of life, in a dusty corridor, a piece of broken china, a stray conversation. We no longer need to climb Sinai to find God; God has descended to ground level, our level. In our spiritual childhood, we imagine that only those things specially marked as "sacred"—a shrine, a prayer, a ritual—speak to us of God. But as we mature, we learn that smaller things—a phone call, a passage in a novel—can be vehicles of love, signs of God's presence. As our understanding deepens, finally it dawns on us that God is everywhere ("the world is charged with the grandeur of God," as Gerard Manley Hopkins so precisely put it).

According to Brother Lawrence, we must consciously strive to greet the world as it comes to us, moment by moment, action by action, person by person. We cease to fret about tomorrow or yesterday; we cease to analyze our behavior; we bid goodbye to daydreams and nightmares; instead, we simply follow the words of the psalmist: "Be still, and know that I am God" (Ps 46:10). In the following passage, Lawrence describes his method in detail and assures us of its plainness:

> The holiest, most ordinary, and most necessary practice of the spiritual life is that of the presence of God. It is to take delight in and become accustomed to his divine company, speaking humbly and conversing lovingly with him all the time, at every moment. . . . We must perform all our actions carefully and deliberately, not impulsively or hurriedly, for such would characterize a distracted mind. We must work gently and lovingly with God.[7]

Lawrence speaks of "conversing lovingly" with God "all the time, at every moment." Yet who can promise this? How can we speak to God unceasingly, day and night, while at the same time maintaining our ordinary activities? What Lawrence suggests, I believe, is the same inner disposition that we seek in the Divine Office and contemplative prayer. Perhaps we can better understand what this asks of us by remembering the New Testament declaration that "God is love" (1 Jn 4:8). God is love and therefore resides wherever love is found. If we perform our daily tasks as Lawrence recommends—that is to say, if we do them lovingly— then we will awaken to the presence of the Love within all love, to the immediacy of God. This idea finds memorable expression in some Italian Renaissance paintings, such as Giotto's *St. Francis Preaching to the Birds*, which depicts the little saint spreading the gospel to a rapt audience of herons, crows, roosters, and other avian catechumens; and Fra Angelico's *Annunciation*, catching the moment when Mary embraces God's love with her own by proclaiming, "Here I am, the servant of the Lord. Let it be with me according to your word" (Lk 1:38). In Mary's speech, in St. Francis's extended arms and open hands, we find just what Brother Lawrence hopes for us all: a stance of love, compassion, and unconditional acceptance.

The practice of the presence unveils a truth of utmost importance for the spiritual life. Many of us believe God to be remote from our lives, a conviction intensified by the pervasive loneliness of modern existence, as well as by the disclosures of science about the vast scale of the universe, the twin abysses of the atom and the stars. But Christianity and the other Abrahamic religions unite in proclaiming the nearness of God. "God is closer to you than your own jugular vein," as the Qur'an has it. We find this truth embodied, as it were, in the biblical image of "the face of God." God is not a remote abstraction; he even possesses a face that we can know and love. Obviously, this is true of Jesus; but it is true also of the Father. "Let the light of your face shine on us, O Lord," declares the psalmist, a plea echoed by all the prophets. Of course, God the Father has no face in the literal sense, yet it would be a great loss to imagine him as faceless, for in this mysterious term, we discern the Father's tender solicitude. God's face—brow of power, eyes of mercy, mouth of justice, countenance of love—turns always toward those who seek his presence. Through Brother Lawrence's practice, we learn to recognize this face, we grow to love its lineaments, glimpsed in the mirror of everyday life.

Throughout the day, then, practice the presence of God. Don't be discouraged if you slip into distraction; just return to your efforts as gently as possible. In order to help you with this practice, I suggest that you choose a "sign"—someone or something that you will encounter several times throughout the day. For example, your sign might be your retreat companion (even the spider that I befriended on that Quaker retreat) or the on/off knob on the kitchen stove. Each time you find yourself face-to-face with your sign—or just thinking of it (or him or her)—drop your work for a moment and try to be aware of God's loving presence. You will find, if you practice diligently, that your efforts will grow stronger, your results more rewarding; prayer has its muscles as well, and they must be kept limber and strong.

TODAY'S PRAYER THEME:
THANKSGIVING

Does it seem strange to offer thanks at the beginning of our retreat? Consider the custom of saying grace: we thank God for our meal before we eat, acknowledging that our food and we who eat it depend on God for our very existence:

O Lord, how manifold are your works!
    In wisdom you have made them all;
    the earth is full of your creatures. . . .
These all look to you
    to give them their food in due season;
When you give it to them, they gather it up;

> when you open your hand, they are filled with good
> things. (Ps 104:24, 27)

Indeed, our retreat itself—an opportunity denied most human beings—can be understood only as a gift from God. So, too, for our wish to go on retreat, our very awareness of spiritual needs and possibilities. God's graciousness toward us began long before we set out for our hermitage; it began, according to scripture, "before the foundation of the world." Our need to give thanks is absolute; it calls, as St. Paul indicates, for an unconditional response:

> Be filled with the spirit, as you sing psalms and hymns and spiritual songs among yourselves, singing and making melody to the Lord in your hearts, giving thanks to God the Father at all times and for everything in the name of our Lord Jesus Christ. (Eph 5:18–20)

Note Paul's emphasis on giving thanks "at all times," strikingly similar to Brother Lawrence's "all the time, at every moment." Given the magnitude of God's gifts, ceaseless gratitude is the only appropriate response.

As Paul's reference to "psalms and hymns and spiritual songs" indicates, we give thanks first and foremost through the Divine Office. But a second means of thanksgiving, mentioned just above, can also play its part. I'm thinking of grace before meals, a custom still practiced in homes that remain aware of our dependence upon divine goodness. Some of my warmest memories revolve around dinners shared with people of other faiths, when the sound of chanted Tibetan, Japanese, Arabic, or Hebrew filled the air, and God's presence seemed as close as my neighbor's. There is no better means of thanking God than saying grace. Through it, we not only express gratitude for the food

upon our table; we also acknowledge its spiritual importance. All religions make much of food, for it binds
together all beings, animal and vegetable. "Give us this
day our daily bread," said Jesus, underscoring its
all-abiding importance. By *daily bread*, Jesus meant
more than processed grain—the term signifies love,
help, supernatural grace—but he meant processed grain
as well. During the Last Supper, bread became the vehicle of Life Eternal; during every supper, it is the agent
of earthly life and a symbol of Christian promise.

Say grace aloud or silently, whichever seems more
suitable. You may use a traditional form, such as:

> Bless us, O Lord,
> and these thy gifts,
> which we are about to receive from thy bounty,
> through Christ our Lord, Amen.

Or you may design your own grace. When my first-
born son John was younger, he liked to add a boyish
spin to his words, giving thanks for the pepperoni top-
ping on the pizza. I suspect that God approved. I pray
that saying grace becomes for you a regular practice, at
least for the duration of the retreat.

Needless to say, thankfulness extends to more than
food. We all know Pollyannas who avert their eyes
from suffering and prattle on about how wonderful life
is. When a Pollyanna gives thanks, her words spring
from ignorance or willful disregard of truth. But there
exists a truly profound type of unalloyed thankfulness,
that of the man or woman who perceives God's graciousness in all events, even in the midst of suffering.
Let us remember Jacques Lusseyran, shouting hosanna in his blindness, shedding light in the darkness of
Buchenwald. Some years ago, I attended a seminar at

Harvard University where the Dalai Lama thanked the Chinese Communists for the 1959 invasion that had wrenched him from the Potala Palace and inflicted so much suffering upon Tibet. From one perspective, these actions of Lusseyran and the Dalai Lama seem incomprehensible, if not perverse, but they admit a deep spiritual truth. As Lusseyran says, everything is "a sign of something else," of God's providence or karmic law, depending upon one's religious vocabulary. Whatever explanation we choose, the same possibility remains: to turn disaster upside down, transforming it, through the power of love, into a reason to give thanks.

FINISHING
THE FIRST DAY

For most people, daily energy crests around noon. By late afternoon or early evening, muscles and motivations sag; we need a second wind. This holds true for the inner life as well; attention flags, prayer practice dwindles to nothing. Sunset is the ideal time to return to contemplation. The more tired you are, the better your prayer will be (as long as you don't fall asleep). Let your weight settle into the chair, use gravity to cement you to the earth, building an immoveable foundation for your practice. You may find your second session of contemplation to be even more rewarding than the first.

Be sure to undertake your silent prayer before dinner— or wait until your food has been digested. During contemplation, your body should do no extraneous work. Once you begin, you'll make a remarkable discovery: Right away, you'll find yourself in the same immutable stillness that you reached in the morning sitting. It will be as if you have returned to a chamber reserved for prayer, a room of silence and tranquility that has become your second home.

After dinner, leave work until tomorrow. Evening lends itself to softer modes of activity, like reading, writing, or listening to music. Once the sun dips below the horizon, our thinking drops into a new register; it slows and deepens, grows more passive, porous, open to subtle influences. But this happens only if we avoid artificial stimulants like alcohol, drugs, or television. These things have no place on retreat.

Now music comes into its own. Choose well. The most obvious possibility, offering both spiritual depth and thematic aptness, is Gregorian chant. Meditative works, like Bach's *B-Minor Mass* or Beethoven's *Late Quartets*, also suit. Avoid popular music that trades in sentimentality, violence, or cheap passion; it will poison your retreat.

As we conclude this first day, I would like to pass on to you a hope, a resolution, and a certainty. The hope is that we feel at home on retreat, for retreat means just that: coming home to self and to God. The resolution is that we use our time well; for we can renew body, mind, and soul, but time cannot be renewed. Each day of this retreat counts. The certainty—which each of us can test for himself or herself—is that the first day of retreat has brought us a small measure of God's peace, and a connection to the great tradition in which we work.

As night closes in, take a few minutes to go over the events of the day, measuring its ups and downs. Don't hesitate to record on paper any insights that have come your way; you will be grateful later for the notes that you keep now. Let us end the day by reflecting on the following paean to prayer—an astonishing cascade of images culminating in two unforgettable last words— by the country parson, metaphysical poet, and great soul George Herbert (1593–1633). In this poem, you'll find all the themes of the day. Read it out loud, just as you read the Divine Office, enunciating each word, listening with all the attention you can muster to the poem's symphony of sound and meaning.

Prayer

Prayer, the Church's banquet, Angels' age,
>   God's breath in man returning to his birth,
The soul in paraphrase, heart in pilgrimage,
>   The Christian plummet, sounding heaven and earth;
Engine against the Almighty, sinner's tower,
>   Reversed thunder, Christ-side-piercing spear,
The six-days' world transposing in an hour,
>   A kind of tune, which all things hear and fear;
Softness, and peace, and joy, and love, and bliss,
>   Exalted manna, gladness of the best,
>   Heaven in ordinary, man well drest,
The milky way, the bird of Paradise,
>   Church-bells beyond the stars heard, the soul's blood,
>   The land of spices; something understood.[8]

cɦapter 5

ᗫAY TWO

THE PATTERN FOR TODAY

Today—Saturday—marks the middle of our sojourn. In the miniature life of this retreat, we are no longer children and not yet elders; this middle position gives us special advantages and challenges. We may receive unexpected insights, but we will also be tested in ways we can't foresee. Having successfully completed the first day, now we may be tempted to take it easy or, conversely, to bear down on ourselves. Instead, let us determine to maintain a steady course, keeping in mind yesterday's promise of stability, which remains valid today. We have taken on what the New Testament calls the yoke (cf. Sanskrit *yoga*) of Christ, a yoke fashioned from love. Let us rejoice, for wearing it will set us free:

> Come to me, all you that are weary and are carrying heavy burdens, and I will give you rest. Take my yoke upon you, and learn from me; for I am gentle and humble in heart, and you will find rest for your souls. For my yoke is easy, and my burden is light. (Mt 11:28–30)

As on Friday, we begin the day with twenty minutes of contemplative prayer (see instructions in chapter 4). Once again, the monastic occupations of Divine Office, *lectio divina*, and manual labor lend stability, balance, and rhythm to our day. We might consider, as a text for *lectio*, the "high priestly prayer" of Jesus (Jn 17:1–25), which has much to say about today's theme of spiritual gestation and transformation. As for manual labor, we need to decide whether to continue with Friday's work or begin a new enterprise. Sustaining yesterday's task allows us to refine skills, remove errors, and perhaps see the job through to completion. On the other hand, we do well to drop any activity that has grown stale, that might tempt us to work distractedly rather than with the awakened attention that we seek.

The Divine Office follows yesterday's pattern. By now you should be well versed in chanting the psalms. If yesterday you recited them silently, out of timidity or bashfulness, today you can speak them aloud, as the authors intended.

THE DIVINE OFFICE FOR
SATURDAY

· $\mathcal{L}$ · A · U · D · S ·

(MORNING OFFICE)

INTRODUCTORY PRAYER

Lord, Open my lips, and my mouth will proclaim your praise.

(*Bow*) Glory be to the Father, and to the Son, and to the Holy Spirit. As it was in the beginning, is now, and ever shall be, world without end, Amen.

MORNING PSALM (PS 119:145–152)

With my whole heart I cry; answer me, O Lord.
> I will keep your statutes.

I cry to you; save me,
> that I may observe your decrees.

I rise before dawn and cry for help;
> I put my hope in your words.

My eyes are awake before each watch of the night,
> that I may meditate on your promise.

In your steadfast love hear my voice;
> O Lord, in your justice preserve my life.

Those who persecute me with evil purpose draw near;
> they are far from your law.

Yet you are near, O Lord,
> and all your commandments are true.

Long ago I learned from your decrees
> that you have established them forever.

(*Bow*) Glory be to the Father, and to the Son, and to the Holy Spirit. As it was in the beginning, is now, and ever shall be, world without end, Amen.

HYMN (EZ 36:26-28)

A new heart I will give you, and a new spirit I will put within you; and I will remove from your body the heart of stone and give you a heart of flesh. I will put my spirit within you, and make you follow my statutes and be careful to observe my ordinances. Then you shall live in the land that I gave to your ancestors, and you shall be my people, and I will be your God.

(*Bow*) Glory be to the Father, and to the Son, and to the Holy Spirit. As it was in the beginning, is now, and ever shall be, world without end, Amen.

PSALM OF PRAISE (PS 8)

O Lord, our Sovereign,
>how majestic is your name in all the earth!

You have set your glory above the heavens.
>Out of the mouths of babes and infants

you have founded a bulwark because of your foes,
>to silence the enemy and the avenger.

When I look at your heavens, the work of your fingers,
>the moon and the stars that you have established;

what are human beings that you are mindful of them,
>mortals that you care for them?

Yet you have made them a little lower than God,
>and crowned them with glory and honor.

You have given them dominion over the works of your hands;
>you have put all things under their feet,

all sheep and oxen,
>and also the beasts of the field,

the birds of the air, and the fish of the sea,
>whatever passes along the paths of the seas.

O Lord, our Sovereign,
>how majestic is your name in all the earth!

(*Bow*) Glory be to the Father, and to the Son, and to the Holy Spirit. As it was in the beginning, is now, and ever shall be, world without end, Amen.

SCRIPTURE READING (ROM 12:14–16A)

Bless those who persecute you; bless and do not curse them. Rejoice with those who rejoice, weep with those who weep. Live in harmony with one another.

SILENT PRAYER

(For a few minutes, we pray to God in silence and stillness. Our prayer may take whatever form suits the moment: thanksgiving, petition, praise, or adoration.)

CANTICLE OF ZECHARIAH (LK 1:68–79)

Blessed be the Lord God of Israel,
>   for he has looked favorably on his people and redeemed
>   them.
He has raised up a mighty savior for us
>   in the house of his servant David,
as he spoke through the mouth of his holy prophets from of old,
>   that we would be saved from our enemies and from the
>   hand of all who hate us.
Thus he has shown the mercy promised to our ancestors,
>   and has remembered his holy covenant,
the oath that he swore to our ancestor Abraham,
>   to grant us that we, being rescued from the hands of our
>   enemies,
might serve him without fear, in holiness and righteousness
>   before him all our days.
And you, child, will be called the prophet of the Most High;
>   for you will go before the Lord to prepare his ways,
to give knowledge of salvation to his people
>   by the forgiveness of their sins.

By the tender mercy of our God,
>the dawn from on high will break upon us,
to give light to those who sit in darkness and in the shadow of
>>death,
>to guide our feet into the way of peace.

(*Bow*) Glory be to the Father, and to the Son, and to the Holy Spirit. As it was in the beginning, is now, and ever shall be, world without end, Amen.

THE LORD'S PRAYER

Our Father, who art in heaven,
>hallowed be thy name.
Thy kingdom come, thy will be done,
>On earth as it is in heaven.
Give us this day our daily bread,
>and forgive us our trespasses,
>as we forgive those who trespass against us.
And lead us not into temptation,
>but deliver us from evil.

CONCLUDING PRAYER

We ask this through Jesus Christ, your Son, who lives and reigns with you and the Holy Spirit, one God forever and ever, Amen.

BLESSING

May the Lord God bless us, guide us, guard us from evil, and bring us to life eternal, Amen.

· V · E · S · P · E · R · S ·

(EVENING OFFICE)

INTRODUCTORY PRAYER

God, come to my assistance; Lord, make haste to help me.

(*Bow*) Glory be to the Father, and to the Son, and to the Holy Spirit. As it was in the beginning, is now, and ever shall be, world without end, Amen.

PSALM (PS 113)

Praise the Lord!
Praise, O servants of the Lord;
    praise the name of the Lord.
Blessed be the name of the Lord
    from this time on and forevermore.
From the rising of the sun to its setting
    the name of the Lord is to be praised.
The Lord is high above all nations,
    and his glory above the heavens.

Who is like the Lord our God,
    who is seated on high,
who looks far down
    on the heavens and the earth?
He raises the poor from the dust,
    and lifts the needy from the ash heap,
to make them sit with princes,
    with the princes of his people.
He gives the barren woman a home,
    making her the joyous mother of children.
Praise the Lord!

(*Bow*) Glory be to the Father, and to the Son, and to the Holy Spirit. As it was in the beginning, is now, and ever shall be, world without end, Amen.

PSALM (PS 16)

Protect me, O God, for in you I take refuge.
I say to the Lord, "You are my Lord;
> I have no good apart from you."

As for the holy ones in the land, they are the noble,
> in whom is all my delight.

Those who choose another god multiply their sorrows;
> their drink offerings of blood I will not pour out
> or take their names upon my lips.

The Lord is my chosen portion and my cup;
> you hold my lot.
The boundary lines have fallen for me in pleasant places;
> I have a goodly heritage.

I bless the Lord who gives me counsel;
> in the night also my heart instructs me.
I keep the Lord always before me;
> because he is at my right hand, I shall not be moved.

Therefore my heart is glad, and my soul rejoices;
> for my body also rests secure.
For you do not give me up to Sheol,
> or let your faithful one see the Pit.

You show me the path of life.
> In your presence there is fullness of joy;
> in your right hand are pleasures forevermore.

(*Bow*) Glory be to the Father, and to the Son, and to the Holy Spirit. As it was in the beginning, is now, and ever shall be, world without end, Amen.

HYMN (PHIL 2:5–9)

Let the same mind be in you that was in Christ Jesus,
who, though he was in the form of God,
> did not regard equality with God

as something to be exploited,
but emptied himself,
>taking the form of a slave,
>being born in human likeness.
And being found in human form,
>he humbled himself
>and become obedient to the point of death—
>even death on a cross.

Therefore God also highly exalted him
>and gave him the name
>that is above every name.

(*Bow*) Glory be to the Father, and to the Son, and to the Holy Spirit. As it was in the beginning, is now, and ever shall be, world without end, Amen.

SCRIPTURE READING (ROM 8:35, 37–39)

Who will separate us from the love of Christ? Will hardship, or distress, or persecution, or famine, or nakedness, or peril, or sword? No, in all these things we are more than conquerors through him who loved us. For I am convinced that neither death, nor life, nor angels, nor rulers, nor things present, nor things to come, nor powers, nor height, nor depth, nor anything else in all creation, will be able to separate us from the love of God in Christ Jesus our Lord.

SILENT PRAYER

(For a few minutes, we pray to God in silence and stillness. Our prayer may take whatever form suits the moment: thanksgiving, petition, praise, or adoration.)

CANTICLE OF MARY (LK 1:46–55)

My soul magnifies the Lord,
>and my spirit rejoices in God my Savior,
for he has looked with favor on the lowliness of his servant.

Surely, from now on all generations will call me blessed;
for the Mighty One has done great things for me,
 and holy is his name.
His mercy is for those who fear him
 from generation to generation.
He has shown strength with his arm;
 he has scattered the proud in the thoughts of their hearts.
He has brought down the powerful from their thrones,
 and lifted up the lowly;
he has filled the hungry with good things,
 and sent the rich away empty.
He has helped his servant Israel,
 in remembrance of his mercy,
according to the promise he made to our ancestors,
 to Abraham and to his descendants forever.

(*Bow*) Glory be to the Father, and to the Son, and to the Holy Spirit. As it was in the beginning, is now, and ever shall be, world without end, Amen.

THE LORD'S PRAYER

Our Father, who art in heaven,
 hallowed be thy name.
Thy kingdom come, thy will be done,
 On earth as it is in heaven.
Give us this day our daily bread,
 and forgive us our trespasses,
 as we forgive those who trespass against us.
And lead us not into temptation,
 but deliver us from evil.

CONCLUDING PRAYER

We ask this through Jesus Christ, your Son, who lives and reigns with you and the Holy Spirit, one God forever and ever, Amen.

BLESSING

May the Lord God bless us, guide us, guard us from evil, and bring us to life eternal, Amen.

· C · O · M · P · L · I · N · E ·

(NIGHT OFFICE)

INTRODUCTORY PRAYER

God, come to my assistance; Lord, make haste to help me.

(*Bow*) Glory be to the Father, and to the Son, and to the Holy Spirit. As it was in the beginning, is now, and ever shall be, world without end, Amen.

EXAMINATION OF CONSCIENCE

(For a few moments, we think back over the day, paying particular attention to any failures in behavior toward ourselves or others. Do we see anything that troubles us in thought or deed? We resolve, simply and gently, to do our best tomorrow.)

PSALM (PS 134)

Come bless the Lord, all you servants of the Lord,
    who stand by night in the house of the Lord!
Lift up your hands to the holy place,
    and bless the Lord.

May the Lord, maker of heaven and earth,
    bless you from Zion.

(*Bow*) Glory be to the Father, and to the Son, and to the Holy Spirit. As it was in the beginning, is now, and ever shall be, world without end, Amen.

SCRIPTURE READING (DT 6:4–7)

Hear, O Israel: the Lord is our God, the Lord alone. You shall love the Lord your God with all your heart, and with all your soul, and with all your might. Keep these words that I am commanding you today in your heart. Recite them to your children and talk about them when you are at home and when you are away, when you lie down and when you rise.

SILENT PRAYER

(For a few minutes, we pray to God in silence and stillness. Our prayer may take whatever form suits the moment: thanksgiving, petition, praise, or adoration.)

CANTICLE OF SIMEON (LK 2:29–32)

Master, now you are dismissing your servant in peace,
        according to your word;
for my eyes have seen your salvation,
        which you have prepared in the presence of all
                peoples,
a light for revelation to the Gentiles
        and for glory to your people Israel.

(Bow) Glory be to the Father, and to the Son, and to the Holy Spirit. As it was in the beginning, is now, and ever shall be, world without end, Amen.

CONCLUDING PRAYER

We pray you Lord, let your holy angels watch over us and let your love be with us always, through Christ our Lord, Amen.

BLESSING

May God grant us a peaceful night, a peaceful death, and perfect peace hereafter.

SALVE REGINA
(A PRAYER TO THE BLESSED VIRGIN MARY)

Hail holy Queen, mother of mercy,
> our life, our sweetness, and our hope.
To you do we cry,
> poor banished children of Eve.
To you do we send up our sighs,
> mourning and weeping in this valley of tears.
Turn then, o most gracious advocate,
> your merciful eyes toward us.
And after this, our exile,
> show to us the blessed fruit of your womb, Jesus.
O clement, o loving, o sweet Virgin Mary.

(The Great Silence descends, not to be broken until the next morning).

TODAY'S THEME:
GESTATION, TRANSFORMATION

I once witnessed a tooth-and-nail argument between two good friends over the nature of enlightenment. Mr. A, a poet much influenced by Zen, argued for instantaneous awakening: liberation, he believed, could come in a flash at any time. Ms. B, a philosopher, vehemently disagreed: spiritual truth, she said, sat atop a mountain that took a lifetime to climb. I enjoyed the debate; the subject was important, and Mr. A and Ms. B both spoke eloquently, although unfortunately they both lost their tempers as the discussion continued. Truth, I reminded myself, is as slippery as a snake, and sooner or later everyone loses his grip. Happily, after a few hours of give-and-take, the two disputants reached a consensus. Let us suppose, they agreed, that truth straddles both positions. Could it be that instant enlightenment is a chimera, that behind it lie years of preparation? And could it be, conversely, that spiritual illumination, however slow the prelude, includes a sudden influx or quantum burst of light?

As this anecdote reveals, today's theme of spiritual gestation turns out—like all real subjects—to be richer and more complex than we usually acknowledge. Just to complicate things a bit more (with an eye toward clarity down the road), let us take a brief hike into the boggy moors of Latin and English grammar. The English verb "to gestate" derives from Latin *gerare*, "to carry." In the time of Shakespeare, people might say "the mother gestates the baby," just as we still say "the mother carries the baby." In this simple declarative sentence, the mother is the subject, the baby the object. Over centuries, however, a surprising linguistic transformation took place, and we now speak of the baby gestating in the womb. The baby has become the subject; its role has become active rather than passive.

At first glance, this observation might seem far removed from our subject, but it tells us a great deal about the monastic meaning of gestation. From a monastic point of view, each of us is an unborn child mothered by God, who bears us, gestates us, and brings us to new birth. At the same time, we carry ourselves toward delivery; we remain responsible for our own development. The work is mutual, and both senses of gestation—ancient and new—apply. We gestate ourselves, and God gestates us. Or, to use a related idiom, we must learn to be both children and adults in relation to God. We need the maturity to become innocents again. Realizing our nature as God's children (and the adult responsibility that this entails) lies at the heart of Jesus' teaching: "Truly I tell you, unless you change and become like children, you will never enter the kingdom of heaven" (Mt 18:3). Paul explains how this is to be done:

> For once you were darkness, but now in the Lord
> you are light. Live as children of light—for the fruit
> of the light is found in all that is good and right and
> true. Try to find out what is pleasing to the Lord."
> (Eph 5:8–10)

Adoption as God's children comes through an ardent search for the good, the right, and the true, an extended gestation in the womb of spiritual discernment. During this process, we shouldn't rely exclusively on ourselves (for our very existence depends on God and we can do nothing without his help), nor should we sit idly by, waiting for God to heal us (for such passivity, epitomized by the Quietists of the seventeenth century, entails a sloughing off of moral effort, a rejection of the freedom and responsibility concomitant with free will). Once again, the Benedictine principle of balance applies.

Here is an exercise to help us appreciate the slow, introspective nature of spiritual growth:

We all realize that our spiritual Aeneid (Ronald Knox's apt phrase, for our spiritual journey is not an odyssey, a return to an old home and an old way of being, but rather an Aeneid, a journey into a new, holier life) didn't begin yesterday morning, when we shut the door against the world and commenced our retreat. Whatever wisdom we find this weekend rests on a foundation built brick-by-brick throughout all the years of our life. Nor did gestation start here; in most cases, our parents prepared the ground for our spiritual formation. Even this description falls short, for our parents' work depended upon that of our grandparents, and so on and so on, back along time's ladder, through the vast sweep of generations flickering in and out of existence over millions of years, until we arrive at the seed itself, in the crude ruttings of Pleistocene protohumans or the chaste loins of Adam and Eve.

Only the tip of this great transgenerational cord of life remains available to us, and even that grows shorter every year. Not so long ago, people could identify their ancestors back five or six generations. Now, few of us can name our great-grandparents. What a terrible loss this collective amnesia is, for family history not only gives us definition; it makes us aware of the tremendous debt we owe our forebears. A million fathers and mothers preceded each of us, a million births about which we know nothing. In a sense, we are the product of a single, great gestation spanning unimaginable epochs, unknown cultures, unnamed ancestors beyond reckoning.

In the face of this boundless generosity, we instinctively turn to yesterday's prayer theme of thanksgiving. I would like to suggest, as an appropriate way to begin, that you spend a few minutes writing down the names of your ancestors, as far back as possible. Your parents will do, if that marks the limit of recall. Consider each name on the list. Let's pick, as an example, your grandfather Antony. If you knew Antony during his lifetime, if he dandled you on his knee or taught you how to drive, bring him to mind as vividly as you can. Remember his voice, his walk, the way he laughed, shook hands, held a cup of coffee. Resurrect him in your memory. Once he stands before you, give him thanks for transmitting life to you. Try to find yourself in him and he in you. Without this man, you would be nothing.

If the name before you is that of a collateral ancestor (cousin, aunt, uncle, etc.), it makes no difference. He or she deserves gratitude all the same; for every ancestor, however remote, shared in the building of the family whose flesh gave birth to you. Nor does it matter if the ancestor died long before you appeared. Here imagination supplants memory, while the task remains the same: to thank those who came before you for the gift of life. Finally, extend your thanks by praying to God for the welfare of the deceased.

TODAY'S PROMISE:

OBEDIENCE

My sixth-grade teacher, whom I will call Mr. Barnstable, a man with a remarkable moustache that flared like rapiers on either side of his face, announced one day that he was dividing our class into two groups for the study of mathematics. One group would consist of advanced pupils; everyone else would be clumped into the "normal" group. To my dismay, Mr. Barnstable plunked me with the normals. For weeks I seethed at this injustice, for I was a lightning-fast calculator and believed that I belonged with the elite. Finally I spoke up. My teacher smiled broadly—a vaguely threatening gesture, as it set his hairy swords abristle—and promised to promote me if I would solve a little problem that, he assured me, "anyone in the advanced group could lick in a minute." To this day I recall the puzzle, for it is burned into a special corner of my brain reserved for painful memories: He asked me to divide 238 by 17. I had never run across long division before.

Instantly, my hopes shattered against the invincible wall of ignorance. Mr. Barnstable looked at me, and I read pity in his eyes. That was the final blow. I dissolved into tears and ran from the room.

For months afterward, I nursed my injured pride. Years passed before I could look at the catastrophe objectively and understand the reason for my failure: I had been undone by my ambition. I had tried to jump over necessary pedagogical steps, disrupting the normal gestation of the mathematical mind. There are laws that need to be followed in the study of mathematics, as in the acquisition of any gift or skill, and I had ignored those laws.

This, I believe, points to the real meaning of obedience, the second promise made by Benedictine monks and nuns upon entering the monastery. Obedience derives from Latin *oboedientia*, which conveys, in addition to the notion of following orders, that of listening. One who obeys is one who listens. (This understanding appears also in Hebrew, which has no verb for "to obey," the act being conveyed by *shama*, "to listen"; in Middle Egyptian, where *shama*, "to listen" + preposition "to" means "to obey"; and perhaps in other ancient or hieratic tongues.) Above all, the monk listens to the abbot and surrenders to his will. In this transaction, the abbot "is believed to hold the place of Christ in the monastery," as Benedict writes in his *Rule* (RB 2). In effect, the monk places himself eagerly, continually, and utterly under God's will—which is holy and pure, while his own is profane and corrupt—by following "the superior's order as promptly as if the command came from God himself." The monk relinquishes the laws of his ego (which instill, *inter alia,* the premature desire to excel at advanced math) and follows the laws of God, by which he gradually matures under the rule of grace into wisdom, purity, and freedom. Ideally, God, abbot, and monk come to share a single will, originating in God, transmitted by the abbot, and executed by the monk. In the first and final stanzas of the *Paradiso*, at the beginning and end of his long, perilous ascent to truth, Dante Alighieri describes the ultimate source of this state of holy obedience:

The glory of the One Who moves all things
        penetrates the universe and shines
        in one part more and in another less. (I:1–3)

Here power failed the highest fantasy;
        but already my desire and will,
     like the wheel spinning in perfect balance,
        were being turned
By the Love that moves the sun and the other stars.
(XXXIII:142–45)

Love powers all: sun, stars, turning wheel. What science calls the law of physics, Christianity calls the law of God, synonymous with love. All things revolve in love and thus in obedience around the Maker of all things. Our lives are no exception. We orbit God by obeying the laws of the spirit. An aboriginal proverb from Australia puts it succinctly: "Human beings are made for the Law, not the Law for human beings." Law, as Chesterton observes in *The Man Who Was Thursday*, is the track that guides the train to its destination. Listen to his poet-policeman declaim with typical Chestertonian paradox upon the theme:

    The rare, strange thing is to hit the mark; the
    gross, obvious thing is to miss it. We feel it is epical
    when man with one wild arrow strikes a distant

bird. Is it not also epical when man with one wild engine strikes a distant station? Chaos is dull, because in chaos the train might indeed go anywhere, to Baker Street or to Baghdad. But man is a magician, and his whole magic is in this, that he does say Victoria, and lo! it is Victoria. No, take your books of mere poetry and prose; let me read a time table, with tears of pride. . . . Every time a train comes in I feel that it has broken past batteries of besiegers, and that man has won a battle against chaos.[1]

May all our trains run on time—but assuredly, they won't. We will enjoy many opportunities to struggle with obedience as our train threatens to derail for any number of reasons, including sloth, despair, and self-love. Today will offer more than its share of disruptions. Be certain of this: difficulties will seek us out. As Martin Luther observed, "a thousand devils hurl themselves against me in my solitude." Once the initial thrill of retreat wears off, we may begin to feel homesick or bored or depressed by our isolation. At this time, obedience becomes a real concern. Do we confront our difficulties or turn away? Stay put or escape?

Many of us will wrestle with contemplative prayer. After five or ten minutes, we may feel a desperate need to stand up, run around, wave our arms, shout hello. Or we may find ourselves growing groggy during the prayer, even nodding off. If difficulties strike, don't cave in. Without a dash of fortitude, we can get nowhere. Many people complain about distraction during contemplation: they plunge into fantastic daydreams, they visit India or Tibet while sitting on their cushions. The only response to such problems is to *stick with it*. Gently return to the task at hand, to the cushion, to the heart, to God.

At times you may be assailed by fear, loneliness, self-pity, or bitterness. Again, my advice is to *stick with it*. In these crises we hear the death-rattle of the ego, a creature who can take a lifetime to die. Be patient. Often reading helps. Or change your activity—go for a walk, cook, listen to music. Write down your feelings and thoughts; this may release some of the pent-up poison. In the final analysis, all these problems boil down to one problem, that of obedience. If we remember our reasons for being where we are, we will forge ahead and even learn to welcome stumbling blocks as opportunities for self-knowledge and self-overcoming (as did Sam when the paint rained down). Some of our best insights come when the world goes haywire, when the chicken blackens in the oven or marsh water soaks the sleeping bag, when we find ourselves frustrated in prayer and foolish in action. For then we see who we really are, and we see in Whom our real hope lies. This marks the beginning of real retreat, real perspective, real prayer. Sometimes these obstacles pile up until we feel arid, useless, utterly spent. God seems absent. Prayer loses its savor. We feel lost, abandoned, out of luck, bereft of hope. In truth, this time of trial—which John of the Cross called "the dark night of the soul"— may prove to be God's greatest gift, an initiation into spiritual maturity, the birth pangs of the new human being. "Take refuge in the Lord," as the Psalmist advises (Ps 5:5), for "the Lord is my rock, my fortress, and my deliverer" (Ps 18:2). Trust in God, and be at peace; God has not forgotten you.

At the same time, obedience means knowing what works and what doesn't. An intelligent runner won't push his leg muscles until they tear. How much truer this should be of us, as we run toward God. I choose this metaphor deliberately, for the Bible teems with images of sprinting: "those who await the Lord . . . shall run and not be weary" (Is 40:31); "Let us run with perseverance the race that is set before us" (Heb 12:1); St. Benedict, in his *Rule,* urges his monks to "run with unspeakable sweetness of love in the way of God's commandments." On this second day of retreat, we find ourselves in the middle of a marathon. This means that we must respect our limits (which is why we withdraw from the world for three days rather than for three years). It also means that, like any athlete, we search out right conditions. In the following passage, Jacques Lusseyran describes the importance to his inner world of a deserted storeroom:

> You can imagine what a big empty room would mean to a blind child. . . . I spent endless hours in the storeroom that summer. I was almost always alone there, but this solitude was densely populated with all kinds of shapes and with the inventions of a personage I had never known before: myself. . . . I was in the state that all children reach sooner or later when, thank heaven, there is no more past or future, no dream or reality, but only themselves riding on life at a gallop.[2]

In this room, Lusseyran discovers stability, freedom, life itself. He comes to this happy state through obedience, by listening to the needs of his imagination and his blindness and finding the right conditions to join the two, so that imagination would heal blindness and blindness set imagination free ("to listen to" and "to do," the twin components of "obey").

Benedictine monasticism employs a particular image to describe this process of self-knowledge through obedience: the ladder of humility. This is a most peculiar ladder, built of the wood of paradox, for on it one descends in order to ascend; as the monk clambers down into greater humility—that is, toward final escape from the selfish ego and its chains—the higher he climbs toward God. By humility, Benedict means something strangely akin to contemplative prayer, a state of being in which we await, in gentle surrender of self-will, the refining fire of God's love. Our surest means of ascent comes by way of the Beatitudes, which counsel mercy over vengeance, meekness over self-assertion, peace over rancor. "Let us love one another," writes the anonymous author of 2 John, who hastens to explain that "this is love, that we walk according to his commandments," thus making explicit the marriage of obedience, humility, and goodness that leads to wisdom. Benedict asks his monks to greet all visitors with a bow; we needn't go this far—although it would do no harm—but certainly we should make every effort to discern Christ's presence in everyone we meet.

A second approach to the ladder of humility comes through self-denial. With this in mind, I would like to suggest an experiment in asceticism. At the mere mention of this word, one or two of you may have fainted dead away. No need to worry; we'll keep the hair shirts and whips in mothballs for another day. Instead, I propose a discipline common to almost all religions: a small fast. This abstinence from over-eating—almost all of us eat too much—can take two forms:

1. Eat only half of your ordinary allotment of food at breakfast, lunch, and dinner.
2. Stop eating between meals.

For most of us, accustomed to munching on cookies or carrots whenever we please, the latter program may be the more arduous of the two. Whichever you choose, I suggest that whenever you feel a pang of hunger, you use it as today's "sign," a summons to rec-ollection, an invitation to prayer. Obviously, this mod-est fast won't catapult you into sanctity. But it is likely to sharpen your attention, lighten your body, and sweeten your mind. In addition, fasting teaches humil-ity, for it highlights our dependence on such lowly things as water and grain, reflections of our final, absolute dependence upon God.

PETITIONARY PRAYER

As we struggle with obstacles, distractions, fears— the intimidating line-up we face every day—sooner or later we will feel overwhelmed. No matter how dili-gently we clear the trail, the brambles surge back. We will never be free of tribulation. For just this reason, we need petitionary prayer.

In this form of prayer, perhaps the most basic of all, we appeal to God for help. He will answer our prayers, as Jesus pledged ("Knock, and the door will be opened for you," Mt 7:7) and as millions of people can attest. However, God responds to our needs, not to our fantasies or fancies. Pray for a cherry-red sports car, and God may answer your prayer by granting you the wis-dom to make a more mature request. Pray for tranquili-ty, and you will receive your share. Nothing could be more certain, for you will soon discover that the act of petition itself brings peace, that it stills the body, soothes the heart, settles the mind, and draws us to

God. Prayers uttered on the verge of life and death—
prayers of a soldier in battle, of a mother in childbirth—
rush us to God, in whose arms we begin to glimpse the
spiritual meaning of suffering. God hears our distress,
whether we know it or not. In ways that we may be too
distraught or blind to discern, God listens and responds.

Don't hesitate to be concrete during prayer; a cherry-
red sports car may be beyond the pale, but we needn't
restrict ourselves to abstractions like peace or love. God,
the Supreme Artist, abhors generalities as much as any
human creator. When Van Gogh dreamt of peace, he
painted a field of Provençal wheat drenched in sunlight.
In the same way, when we ask for serenity, we do well
to translate our wish into specifics. Pray for what will
bring you real peace: the courage to control your anger,
or the good health to begin a new job. If all this seems
too audacious, you might petition a favorite saint to
intercede for you with God. Many Catholics in dire
straits petition St. Jude, patron of hopeless causes (no
one knows how poor Jude received this onerous job,
although the similarity of his name to that of Judas
Iscariot suggests a case of mistaken identity). Such a
prayer may be as simple as "St. Jude, fly to my assistance. Ask God to help me with [fill in the blank]." Such
a pure prayer is certain to reach God's ears.

TODAY'S PRAYER PRACTICE:
THE JESUS PRAYER

One late autumn day in the mid-nineteenth century, a man with a withered arm set out across Russia in
search of the secret of perfect prayer. He carried
nothing but his Bible, a few husks of bread, and an
invincible longing for God. At first his mission seemed

hopeless. He begged for instruction in every town but received only lofty sermons, filled with platitudes, from priests and laypeople alike. But the pilgrim hungered for more than eloquent abstractions; he sought a sure method to bring him to God. Eventually he encountered a *staretz*—a church elder—who offered him what he sought, in the form of the "Jesus Prayer": a continual repetition of the words "Lord Jesus Christ, Son of God, have mercy on me, a sinner." This prayer changed the pilgrim's life:

> Sometimes my heart would feel as though it were bubbling with joy; such lightness, freedom, and consolation were in it. Sometimes I felt a burning love for Jesus Christ and for all God's creatures. Sometimes my eyes brimmed over with tears of thankfulness to God, who was so merciful to me, a wretched sinner. . . . Sometimes by calling upon the name of Jesus I was overwhelmed with bliss, and now I knew the meaning of the words, "The Kingdom of God is within you."[3]

For several years the pilgrim wandered the land, continuing to practice the Jesus Prayer. Every trial he encountered became a lesson in grace. He was exiled, flogged, and nearly died after a fall into icy waters. Once a wolf attacked him before recognizing his holiness and running away. These sufferings, far from discouraging him, deepened his faith in Christ and his reliance upon the Prayer. The Jesus Prayer, he told all who would listen, bestowed "understanding of Holy Scripture, knowledge of the speech of created things, freedom from fuss and vanity, knowledge of the joy of the inner life, and finally certainty of the nearness of God and of His love for us."[4]

A century and a half later, the story of this anonymous Russian pilgrim continues to fascinate (it even achieved fleeting literary notoriety during the 1960s, when J. D. Salinger made the Jesus Prayer the centerpiece of his best-selling novella, *Franny and Zooey*). Yet the prayer's longevity depends not upon cultural trends but upon the simplicity and integrity of its form. The Jesus Prayer is petitionary prayer at its purest. We simply ask God, in the person of Jesus Christ, for mercy; in so doing, we acknowledge faith in his power, wisdom, and love. In effect, the Jesus Prayer is Christianity compressed into twelve words. Some Orthodox hesychast (*hesychia* = Greek for "tranquility") theologians believe that the Prayer bestows upon its practitioners "divine energies," a term that may be loosely defined as God's manifest presence. When we pray the Jesus Prayer, it has been said, God prays with us; heaven and earth unite in holy invocation. According to tradition, the Prayer derives its power from the numinous power of God's name (revealed to Moses during his Sinai retreat); its form from the passage in Luke (18:35–43) in which a blind man from Jericho shouts out "Jesus, Son of David, have mercy on me!" and regains his sight; and its prestige from Jesus' promise that "if you ask anything of the Father in my name, he will give it to you" (Jn 16:23).

At first, the Jesus Prayer should be said slowly and distinctly, heeding the meaning of each word, just as we recite the Divine Office. Repeat the Prayer often; the pilgrim reports saying it six thousand times a day! To keep count, many people use a prayer rope, a simple woolen string divided into fifty or one hundred knots (see chapter 3). In some Orthodox monasteries, monks accompany each repetition with a deep bow or even a full prostration, forehead to floor. It may be best to avoid such exertions during our brief retreat. However, I encourage you to say the Prayer in all circumstances: walking, driving, sewing, rocking a baby. Pray out loud, subvocalize the words, or sound them in your heart.

The Jesus Prayer can become a lifelong practice. Eventually, you may notice something unusual taking place: the pilgrim reports, and others confirm, that after a while the Prayer becomes self-acting, moving from the conscious to the subconscious, then from the mind into the heart (that is, from the intellectual center into the center of our being) until finally one recites it at all times, awake or asleep. Most of us, however, will find that our practice of the Prayer ebbs and flows, or even dries up altogether—offering us another lesson in humility and another chance to begin again.

FINISHING
THE DAY

I recommend that we complete the second day of our retreat as we did the first, with contemplative prayer, Compline, and quiet recreation. To add variety to this program, here is a small experiment in self-examination to round off the evening: Begin by making a list of your "enemies," those people whom you avoid or dislike. You needn't come up with anyone who sends you into cardiac arrest; think of someone whose face you find unpleasant or whose political beliefs you scorn. Then remember how the Dalai Lama treated China, the nation that invaded and ravaged his native land (see chapter 4). Each person on your list is your "China": an apparent enemy that needs to be transformed, through humility and with God's help, into a genuine friend.

Dwell on each person in turn. Picture this woman—an old business associate who talks when she should listen and never follows your advice—as she eats dinner, tucks her children into bed, takes Rover for a romp. Does her image arouse pity, anger, envy? All such feelings play a part in our dislike of another. If you suddenly switched your life with hers, how would you react? Can you see the justice of her ways? How do you suppose she looks at you? What now of your judgments, your condemnations?

Carry this exercise one step further. Death, the great leveler, is the great leaven as well. In the face of death—even an exercise in imaginary death—we may rise to new heights of love and understanding. People close to God value reminders of death: thus the black of the Benedictine habit, the tombstone-shaped hats of Islamic dervishes, and the ascetic practice (found in Christianity, Buddhism, and other religions) of picturing as vividly as possible the decay of one's corpse. Imagine each of your so-called enemies on the brink of death, calling out to you for help. How will you respond? What resources of love do their cries summon?

Let us end Saturday by meditating on two prayer-poems, each a model of petition. The first is a hymn from medieval England; the second, a composition by novelist Jane Austen (1775–1817). Again, I advise you to read each poem aloud, slowly and reflectively.

Hymn

God be in my hede
    And in my understandyng,
God be in myne eyes
    And in my loking,
God be in my mouth
    And in my speaking,
God be in my harte
    And in my thynkyng,
God be in mine ende
    And at my departyng.

    ~ Anonymous[5]

Prayer

Incline us O God! to think humbly of ourselves, to be saved only in the examination of our own conduct, to consider our fellow-creatures with kindness, and to judge of all they say and do with the charity which we would desire from them ourselves.

    ~ Jane Austen[6]

chapter 6

$\mathcal{D}$AY THREE

THE PATTERN FOR TODAY

Sunday, the day of resurrection, marks the coming-of-age of our retreat. Planting and pruning are at an end; today, the tree bears fruit. Let us take the time to gather a full harvest. Perhaps we are already looking ahead to tonight or tomorrow, when we will return to ordinary life. Or perhaps we are casting a jaundiced eye over the last two days. Future and past tug at our sleeve. I suggest that we respond to these distractions with an extraordinary effort of recollection in all our prayers, labors, and exercises. Let us, as Thoreau advised, "live deeply and suck out all the marrow."

We begin, as always, with twenty minutes of contemplation. Today we will pay particular attention to our state immediately after leaving the prayer. What is this tranquility that we feel in bones and blood as well as in mind? What sustains it? What steals it away? Perhaps we can learn a little more about the nature of contemplative prayer and how to integrate it into our ordinary lives by seeing how its qualities evaporate when we arise from contemplation.

Once again, the Divine Office marks the phases of the day. The texts can be found below. For today's *lectio divina,* consider meditating upon the parable of the prodigal son (Lk 15:11–32), which has much to say about today's theme. As for manual labor, finish yesterday's work or begin something new, but bear in mind that our retreat ends this evening; this isn't the time to start a long-range project.

THE DIVINE OFFICE FOR SUNDAY

· *L* · A · U · D · S ·

(MORNING OFFICE)

INTRODUCTORY PRAYER

Lord, Open my lips, and my mouth will proclaim your praise.

(*Bow*) Glory be to the Father, and to the Son, and to the Holy Spirit. As it was in the beginning, is now, and ever shall be, world without end, Amen.

MORNING PSALM (PS 63:1–8)

O God, you are my God, I seek you
    my soul thirsts for you;
my flesh faints for you,
    as in a dry and weary land where there is no water.

So I have looked upon you in the sanctuary,
>   beholding your power and glory.
Because your steadfast love is better than life,
>   my lips will praise you.
So I will bless you as long as I live;
>   I will lift up my hands and call on your name.
My soul is satisfied as with a rich feast,
>   and my mouth praises you with joyful lips
when I think of you on my bed,
>   and meditate on you in the watches of the night;
for you have been my help,
>   and in the shadow of your wings I sing for joy.
My soul clings to you;
>   your right hand upholds me.

(*Bow*) Glory be to the Father, and to the Son, and to the Holy Spirit. As it was in the beginning, is now, and ever shall be, world without end, Amen.

HYMN (DN 3:52–57; ALSO KNOWN AS THE PRAYER OF AZARIAH, 29–34)

Blessed are you, O Lord, God of our ancestors,
>   and to be praised and highly exalted forever;
And blessed is your glorious, holy name,
>   and to be highly praised and highly exalted forever.
Blessed are you in the temple of your holy glory,
>   and to be extolled and highly glorified forever.
Blessed are you who look into the depths from your throne on
>   the cherubim,
>   and to be praised and highly exalted forever.
Blessed are you on the throne of your kingdom,
>   and to be extolled and highly exalted forever.
Blessed are you in the firmament of heaven,
>   and to be sung and glorified forever.

(*Bow*) Glory be to the Father, and to the Son, and to the Holy Spirit. As it was in the beginning, is now, and ever shall be, world without end, Amen.

PSALM OF PRAISE (PS 148)

Praise the Lord!
Praise the Lord from the heavens;
 praise him in the heights!
Praise him, all his angels,
 praise him, all his host!

Praise him, sun and moon;
 praise him, all you shining stars!
Praise him, you highest heavens,
 and you waters above the heavens!

Let them praise the name of the Lord,
 for he commanded and they were created.
He established them forever and ever;
 he fixed their bounds, which cannot be passed.

Praise the Lord from the earth,
 you sea monsters and all deeps,
fire and hail, snow and frost,
 stormy wind fulfilling his command!

Mountains and all hills,
 fruit trees and all cedars!
Wild animals and all cattle,
 creeping things and flying birds!

Kings of the earth and all peoples,
 princes and all rulers of the earth!
Young men and women alike,
 old and young together!
Let them praise the name of the Lord,
 for his name alone is exalted;
 his glory is above earth and heaven.

He has raised up a horn for his people,

>   praise for all his faithful,

>   for the people of Israel who are close to him.

Praise the Lord!

(*Bow*) Glory be to the Father, and to the Son, and to the Holy Spirit. As it was in the beginning, is now, and ever shall be, world without end, Amen.

SCRIPTURE READING (EZ 37:12–14)

Thus says the Lord God: I am going to open your graves, and bring you up from your graves, O my people; and I will bring you back to the land of Israel. And you shall know that I am the Lord, when I open your graves, and bring you up from your graves, O my people. I will put my spirit within you, and you shall live, and I will place you on your own soil; then you shall know that I, the Lord, have spoken and will act.

SILENT PRAYER

(For a few minutes, we pray to God in silence and stillness. Our prayer may take whatever form suits the moment: thanksgiving, petition, praise, or adoration.)

CANTICLE OF ZECHARIAH (LK 1:68–79)

Blessed be the Lord God of Israel,

>   for he has looked favorably on his people and redeemed
>   them.

He has raised up a mighty savior for us

>   in the house of his servant David,

as he spoke through the mouth of his holy prophets from of old,

that we would be saved from our enemies and from the hand

>   of all who hate us.

Thus he has shown the mercy promised to our ancestors,

>   and has remembered his holy covenant,

the oath that he swore to our ancestor Abraham,
  to grant us that we, being rescued from the hands of our
      enemies,
might serve him without fear, in holiness and righteousness
  before him all our days.
And you, child, will be called the prophet of the Most High;
  for you will go before the Lord to prepare his ways,
to give knowledge of salvation to his people
  by the forgiveness of their sins.
By the tender mercy of our God,
  the dawn from on high will break upon us,
to give light to those who sit in darkness and in the shadow of
      death,
  to guide our feet into the way of peace.

(*Bow*) Glory be to the Father, and to the Son, and to the Holy
Spirit. As it was in the beginning, is now, and ever shall be,
world without end, Amen.

THE LORD'S PRAYER

Our Father, who art in heaven,
  hallowed be thy name.
Thy kingdom come, thy will be done,
  On earth as it is in heaven.
Give us this day our daily bread,
  and forgive us our trespasses,
 as we forgive those who trespass against us.
And lead us not into temptation,
  but deliver us from evil.

CONCLUDING PRAYER

We ask this through Jesus Christ, your Son, who lives and
reigns with you and the Holy Spirit, one God forever and ever,
Amen.

BLESSING

May the Lord God bless us, guide us, guard us from evil, and bring us to life eternal, Amen.

· V · E · S · P · E · R · S ·

(E V E N I N G   O F F I C E)

INTRODUCTORY PRAYER

God, come to my assistance; Lord, make haste to help me.

(*Bow*) Glory be to the Father, and to the Son, and to the Holy Spirit. As it was in the beginning, is now, and ever shall be, world without end, Amen.

PSALM (PS 110:2-4)

The Lord sends out from Zion
>your mighty scepter.
>Rule in the midst of your foes.
Your people will offer themselves willingly
>on the day you lead your forces
>on the holy mountains.
From the womb of the morning,
>like dew, your youth will come to you.

(*Bow*) Glory be to the Father, and to the Son, and to the Holy Spirit. As it was in the beginning, is now, and ever shall be, world without end, Amen.

PSALM (PS 111)

Praise the Lord!
I will give thanks to the Lord with my whole heart,
>in the company of the upright, in the congregation.
Great are the works of the Lord,

studied by all who delight in them.
Full of honor and majesty is his work,
     and his righteousness endures forever.
He has gained renown by his wonderful deeds;
     the Lord is gracious and merciful.
He provides food for those who fear him;
     he is ever mindful of his covenant.
He has shown his people the power of his works,
     in giving them the heritage of the nations.
The work of his hands are faithful and just;
     all his precepts are trustworthy.
They are established forever and ever,
     to be performed with faithfulness and uprightness.
He sent redemption to his people;
     he has commanded his covenant forever.
     Holy and awesome is his name.
The fear of the Lord is the beginning of wisdom;
     all those who practice it have a good understanding.
     His praise endures forever.

(*Bow*) Glory be to the Father, and to the Son, and to the Holy Spirit. As it was in the beginning, is now, and ever shall be, world without end, Amen.

HYMN (RV 19:1-2, 5-8)

Hallelujah!
Salvation and glory and power to our God,
for his judgments are true and just.
Praise our God, all you his servants,
and all who fear him, small and great.
For the Lord our God the Almighty reigns.
Let us rejoice and exult and give him the glory.
For the marriage of the Lamb has come,
and his bride has made herself ready.

(*Bow*) Glory be to the Father, and to the Son, and to the Holy Spirit. As it was in the beginning, is now, and ever shall be, world without end, Amen.

SCRIPTURE READING (2 THES 2:13–14)

We must always give thanks to God for you, brothers and sisters beloved by the Lord, because God chose you as the first fruits for salvation through sanctification by the Spirit and through belief in the truth. For this purpose he called you through our proclamation of the good news, so that you may obtain the glory of our Lord Jesus Christ.

SILENT PRAYER

(For a few minutes, we pray to God in silence and stillness. Our prayer may take whatever form suits the moment: thanksgiving, petition, praise, or adoration.)

CANTICLE OF MARY (LK 1:46–55)

My soul magnifies the Lord,
  and my spirit rejoices in God my Savior,
for he has looked with favor on the lowliness of his servant.
  Surely, from now on all generations will call me blessed;
for the Mighty One has done great things for me,
  and holy is his name.
His mercy is for those who fear him
  from generation to generation.
He has shown strength with his arm;
  he has scattered the proud in the thoughts of their hearts.
He has brought down the powerful from their thrones,
  and lifted up the lowly;
he has filled the hungry with good things,
  and sent the rich away empty.
He has helped his servant Israel,

in remembrance of his mercy,
according to the promise he made to our ancestors,
to Abraham and to his descendants
forever.

(Bow) Glory be to the Father, and to the Son, and to the Holy Spirit. As it was in the beginning, is now, and ever shall be, world without end, Amen.

THE LORD'S PRAYER

Our Father, who art in heaven,
hallowed be thy name.
Thy kingdom come, thy will be done,
On earth as it is in heaven.
Give us this day our daily bread,
and forgive us our trespasses,
as we forgive those who trespass against us.
And lead us not into temptation,
but deliver us from evil.

CONCLUDING PRAYER

We ask this through Jesus Christ, your Son, who lives and reigns with you and the Holy Spirit, one God forever and ever, Amen.

BLESSING

May the Lord God bless us, guide us, guard us from evil, and bring us to life eternal, Amen.

· C · O · M · P · L · I · N · E ·

(NIGHT OFFICE)

INTRODUCTORY PRAYER

God, come to my assistance; Lord, make haste to help me.

(*Bow*) Glory be to the Father, and to the Son, and to the Holy Spirit. As it was in the beginning, is now, and ever shall be, world without end, Amen.

EXAMINATION OF CONSCIENCE

(For a few moments, we think back over the day, paying particular attention to any failures in behavior toward ourselves or others. Do we see anything that troubles us in thought or deed? We resolve, simply and gently, to do our best tomorrow.)

PSALM (PS 91)

You who live in the shelter of the Most High,
>who abide in the shadow of the Almighty,
will say to the Lord, "My refuge and my fortress;
>my God, in whom I trust."
For he will deliver you from the snare of the fowler
>and from the deadly pestilence;
he will cover you with his pinions,
>and under his wings you will find refuge;
>his faithfulness is a shield and buckler.
You will not fear the terror of the night,
>or the arrow that flies by day,
or the pestilence that stalks in darkness,
>or the destruction that wastes at noonday.

A thousand may fall at your side,
>ten thousand at your right hand,
>but it will not come near you.

You will only look with your eyes
    and see the punishment of the wicked.

Because you have made the Lord your refuge,
    the Most High your dwelling place,
no evil shall befall you,
    no scourge come near your tent.

For he will command his angels concerning you
    to guard you in all your ways.
On their hands they will bear you up,
    so that you will not dash your foot against a stone.
You will tread on the lion and the adder,
    the young lion and the serpent you will trample under
        foot.

Those who love me, I will deliver;
    I will protect those who know my name.
When they call to me, I will answer them;
    I will be with them in trouble,
    I will rescue them and honor them,
With long life I will satisfy them,
    and show them my salvation.

(*Bow*) Glory be to the Father, and to the Son, and to the Holy Spirit. As it was in the beginning, is now, and ever shall be, world without end, Amen.

SCRIPTURE READING (REV 22:4–5)

His servants will worship him; they will see his face, and his name will be on their foreheads. And there will be no more night; they need no light of lamp or sun, for the Lord God will be their light, and they will reign forever and ever.

SILENT PRAYER

(For a few minutes, we pray to God in silence and stillness. Our prayer may take whatever form suits the moment: thanksgiving, petition, praise, or adoration.)

CANTICLE OF SIMEON (LK 2:29-32)

Master, now you are dismissing your servant in peace,
    according to your word;
for my eyes have seen your salvation,
    which you have prepared in the presence of all peoples,
a light for revelation to the Gentiles
    and for glory to your people Israel.

(Bow) Glory be to the Father, and to the Son, and to the Holy Spirit. As it was in the beginning, is now, and ever shall be, world without end, Amen.

CONCLUDING PRAYER

We pray you Lord, let your holy angels watch over us and let your love be with us always, through Christ our Lord, Amen.

BLESSING

May God grant us a peaceful night, a peaceful death, and perfect peace hereafter.

SALVE REGINA
(A PRAYER TO THE BLESSED VIRGIN MARY)

Hail holy Queen, mother of mercy,
    our life, our sweetness, and our hope.
To you do we cry,
    poor banished children of Eve.
To you do we send up our sighs,
    mourning and weeping in this valley of tears.
Turn then, o most gracious advocate,

your merciful eyes toward us.
And after this, our exile,
    show to us the blessed fruit of your womb, Jesus.
O clement, o loving, o sweet Virgin Mary.

(The Great Silence descends, not to be broken until the next morning).

TODAY'S THEME:
RESURRECTION

In 1933, a fisherman working the waters off the Comoro Islands in the Indian Ocean hooked something utterly unexpected, a stubby fish five feet long, with spherical scales, steel-blue body, lobed tail, and vestigial lungs. The catch soon caught the world's attention, and not only because of the creature's implausible appearance, which resembled a beast from a Brueghelian nightmare. Still more astonishing was the fish's identity, for a search through the icythyo-paleontological literature proved it to be a coelacanth, a species recognized only from the fossil record and believed to have died out 350 million years ago. This "living fossil" brought to the world the same shiver of wonder that we experience when the first crocus breaks through its casket of snow and winter's privations give way to spring's bounty: the astonishment of resurrection.

On every Sunday of the year, Christians around the world celebrate the prototype of all resurrection, that of Jesus Christ. St. Paul describes the Resurrection of Christ and our own future resurrection in these terms:

> What is sown is perishable, what is raised is imperishable. It is sown in dishonor, it is raised in glory. It is sown in weakness, it is raised in power. It is sown a physical body, it is raised a spiritual body (1 Cor 15:42–44).

Resurrection is more than repetition, more than starting afresh; it is awakening to a new order of being. Our retreat offers the possibility of a foretaste of this overwhelming event. On Friday, we made an effort to break the chains of the past. On Saturday, we nourished our resolve in the womb of silence, stillness, and peace. Now, on Sunday, we can begin to "walk in newness of life" as "children of God, and if children, then heirs" (Rom 6:14, 9:17), inheritors of one of God's greatest gifts, the transformation of being that lies at the center of the Christian life. In order to understand more of what this signifies, let us turn now to the last of the three Benedictine vows, that of *conversio*.

TODAY'S PROMISE:
CONVERSIO

As said above, when Greek Orthodox monks chant the Jesus Prayer, they sometimes accompany it with a full prostration, forehead touching the ground. The monks call this movement *metanoia,* a Greek term that means "change of mind." As one can see, "mind" here has a rather broad definition, for it includes within it the action of the body. And the heart participates as well, for prostration is a gesture of humility, a confession of our dependence upon and love for God. Heart, body, mind, and spirit: the entire human being participates in *metanoia.* For this reason, the word is appropriately translated not simply as "change of mind," but, more richly, as "change of being."

Metanoia, or *conversio,* as Benedictines call it, is the third vow made by a monk or nun upon entering the monastery. We will make it the focus of today's inner work. In truth, however, this striving toward God through self-transformation lies at the base of our entire retreat and indeed of our entire spiritual and religious life. The many concerns of Friday and Saturday—thanksgiving and petition, stability and obedience, the practice of the presence and the Jesus Prayer—all participate in the work of *conversio*. It underlies every aspect of monastic profession. Listen to this assessment by Thomas Merton, delivered to an assembly of Benedictine abbots in Thailand just a few hours before his death:

> When you stop and think a little bit about St. Benedict's concept of *conversatio morum*, that most mysterious of our vows, which is actually the most essential I believe, it can be interpreted as a commitment to total inner transformation of one sort or another—a commitment to become a completely new man. It seems to me that that could be regarded as the end of the monastic life, and that no matter where one attempts to do this, that remains the essential thing.[1]

The call to *conversio* rings throughout the New Testament. We encounter it first in the summons of John the Baptist: "Repent, for the kingdom of heaven is at hand" (Mt 3:2). Repentance, which has accrued such negative connotations in modern usage, originally meant just this supreme transformation of being from darkness to light, ignorance to knowledge, hate to love. Jesus' entire teaching can be summed up as a summons to *conversio*, in which the Beatitudes define both the qualities that initiate transformation and the blessings that ensue:

Blessed are the poor in spirit, for theirs is the kingdom of
heaven.
Blessed are those who mourn, for they will be comforted.
Blessed are the meek, for they will inherit the earth.
Blessed are those who hunger and thirst for righteousness, for
they will be filled.
Blessed are the merciful, for they will receive mercy.
Blessed are the pure in heart, for they will see God.
Blessed are the peacemakers, for they will be called children
of God. (Mt 5:3–10)

To many people, *conversio* implies a sudden, breath-taking change in identity. An outstanding example of such a makeover occurs in Charles Dickens's *A Christmas Carol*. When Ebenezer Scrooge awakens on December 25 after a night of visions, the first words to soar from his mouth are "I am not the man I was." He has followed Paul's counsel in Ephesians 4:22–24:

> to put away your former way of life, your old self,
> corrupt and deluded by its lusts, and to be renewed
> in the spirit of your minds, and to clothe yourselves
> with the new self, created according to the likeness
> of God in true righteousness and holiness.

Donning a new self overnight can change the world; think of the indelible effect of St. Francis's *conversio* on medieval Europe. However, radical transformations like these are rare. God generously offers most of us another path to sanctity: the humble, muted *conversio* that we are asked to undertake each moment of our lives. This is the *conversio* of which St. Benedict writes. As with other Benedictine vows, we do well to seek help from the saints in order to understand how we may embrace *conversio* in our own lives. Who among the saints best exemplifies this gentle way of transformation? A blazing comet like St. Francis, who kissed lepers, communed with angels, and preached to birds, may be too extraordinary for our needs. Let us turn to someone more like ourselves, at least in outward circumstances. I believe that, in our efforts at conversion, we can learn much from the well-fed, elegantly dressed, snugly housed, headstrong, somewhat spoiled girl who became St. Thérèse of Lisieux, founder of the "little way."

What background can rival Thérèse's for coziness? She was the youngest of five daughters, born to a devout, well-to-do watchmaker and his doting wife, a family submerged in the plush silk-and-brocade comforts of late nineteenth-century French bourgeois life. Only one feature disturbs the banal composition of the scene: From an early age, Thérèse harbored an unshakeable determination to "enter Carmel," the Order of Discalced Carmelites, the same religious society to which Brother Lawrence had belonged. To fulfill what she insisted was God's will, the girl concocted some audacious schemes, the most outrageous unfolding on a visit to Rome in 1887, when she breached the code of silence during an audience with Pope Leo XIII to whisper in his ear, "Holy Father, in honor of your Jubilee, permit me to enter Carmel at the age of fifteen." Not surprisingly, the Pope replied, "I don't understand very well." When the matter was explained, he sensibly assured Thérèse that "you will enter if God wills it."[2] And so God did, four months later.

This unexceptional girl, whose spunk puts us more in mind of Nancy Drew than someone of exalted sanctity, entered the Carmel at Lisieux, France, in 1888. She never again left the monastery grounds; guests spoke to her through an iron grille (put in place, you will recall, not to keep the nuns in but to keep the world out). Eight years after her entrance, on Good Friday, 1896, Thérèse coughed up blood. The diagnosis was tuberculosis. Seventeen months later, on September 30, 1897, she died at the age of twenty-four.

Thérèse has been called "the greatest saint of modern times," a designation bestowed on her by Pius XI and seconded by millions of devotees. What did she do, in those nine years in the monastery, to earn this accolade? On the surface of things, next to nothing, apart from writing her autobiography on the orders of her Mother Superior. For Thérèse sought God not in grand cataclysms but in the smallest of events (folding laundry, polishing the silverware) and in the absence of events, the silences that fill the interstices of our lives. Here, we hearken back to Brother Lawrence's practice of the presence. We have come full circle. But the circle proves to be a spiral, for Thérèse carries us one step further along and higher up the path toward God. In her "little way," we find the continual awareness of God's presence expressed in a new, more radical mode. Thérèse makes explicit what lies implicit in Brother Lawrence's method and in all Christian practice: utter abandonment to love. She wrote many passages proclaiming her surrender to love, but none more fervent than these in her June 9, 1895, "Act of Oblation to Merciful Love," addressed directly to God:

> In order to live in one single act of perfect Love, I offer myself as a victim of holocaust to your merciful love, asking you to consume me incessantly, allowing the waves of infinite tenderness shut up within You to overflow into my soul. . . . I want, O my Beloved, at each beat of my heart to renew this offering to You an infinite number of times.[3]

Underneath this purple passion lies a revolutionary truth, expressed in Thérèse's promise to renew her love "at each beat of my heart." According to Thérèse, true love—and the true *conversio* that leads to it—does not demand spectacular public sacrifice (as in the literal holocaust that consumed St. Joan of Arc, whose death at the stake Thérèse once portrayed in a play put on at the Lisieux Carmel). It may simply require putting the forks, knives, and spoons away in their proper order. As an adolescent, Thérèse dreamed of a Joan-like martyrdom; genuine *conversio*, she discovered as an adult, lay in sweeping away these fantasies and turning instead to the plain, hard work of sweeping the convent floors. At "each beat of [the] heart," Thérèse teaches, by attending faithfully to the task before us, we may turn from self-will toward the will of God. In this process lie the root, trunk, and branch of real humility, real maturity, real *conversio*.

So far on this retreat, I have shied away from talking about morality. This caution makes sense, I believe, for discussions about morals can easily degenerate into carping, knuckle-rapping, or bombast. I have neither the wish nor the expertise to write guidelines for the moral life; God did the job rather well in sacred scripture. However, no presentation of *conversio* can afford to skate around the issue, for spiritual transformation never takes place in a void, but in a landscape of moral decisions that affect not only ourselves but others, near and far. In the last analysis, the depth of our *conversio* may depend upon how we respond to moral choices.

Bearing these considerations in mind, I suggest that we leap over specific issues and explore the source of all moral decisions, that mysterious presence that we commonly call "conscience." Few people agree on what conscience is or how it comes to prick us with such gusto; nonetheless, we all know it when we feel it—that inner prod that tells us, often in the face of burning desire, to do this or to refrain from doing that. Conscience seems to be an organ, like eyes or ears, that part of ourselves that perceives good and evil and that guides us toward the good. Something of God dwells in conscience. We may call it a whisper from heaven, or God's yeast at work in the world.

Whatever metaphor we choose to describe conscience, we all know the difficulties of listening and responding to its promptings (here again, we find "to listen" and "to do": by following conscience, we wed yesterday's promise of obedience to today's of *conversio*). Certainly, our task demands more than adherence to local codes of behavior, which may sanction activities that cut our conscience badly. Nor, as I think we all recognize, can we simply do whatever feels good. Neither indulgence nor passivity will lead us to conscience. Once again, St. Benedict's principle of moderation lights the way. To know our conscience, we must cultivate a mature relationship to our desires. The body's ceaseless clamorings—for sex, for sleep, for food—need to be kept in check, lest we perish like those laboratory rats who, offered unlimited quantities of sugar, eat until they burst. We need to harness our carnal appetites to our higher hunger for health, love, and union with God. If we do so, eventually a new voice sounds within us, that of the awakened conscience: faint and frail at first, so tiny a thing that we see how right Walt Disney was to personify it as a cricket. Only gradually, by fits and starts, do we become able to follow Jiminy's counsel "to let your conscience be your guide."

As an experiment in *conversio*, including its moral dimension, I propose that you draw up a list of everything that you would like to change about yourself. Your catalog should include physical improvements, such as losing weight or building up stamina; mental improvements, like learning Japanese or reading Homer; and moral improvements, such as corking your temper or your inclination to belittle others. Once you have completed your list, select one item—*only one*—on which to work. Choose something important (not to find a better hair rinse) and something doable (not to be free from anger at all times). From now on, let this become your goal. Work on it every day without fail. Be patient with this task. Whatever your goal, almost certainly you will backslide repeatedly. No matter: God's patience will outlast your own. You will soon discover that your ambition has become the flagship for a flotilla of other longed-for changes in your life. Combat of this sort enhances rather than depletes inner strength; when we tackle one resolution, we find the power to wrestle with the next. This process, in which one virtue imparts life to another, helps us to grasp the wisdom in Jesus' demand, so terrifying at first glance, to "be perfect, therefore, as your heavenly Father is perfect" (Mt 5:48). All *conversio* tends toward perfection. That we will never attain this state doesn't matter—or rather, it matters more than anything, for it means that we always have a goal toward which to strive.

TODAY'S PRAYER THEMES:
ADORATION AND PRAISE

What do we mean by adoration, the first of today's intertwined prayer themes? It derives from *adorare*,

Latin for "to pray to," an embellishment of *orare*, originally "to speak." Adoration is thus intimately linked to speech, the fundamental act by which we go beyond ourselves to meet the world. Recall the moment in the 1962 film *The Miracle Worker* when little Helen Keller—locked since infancy in the solitary confinement of her own body, with iron bars across her eyes, ears, and mouth—discovers language while running her fingers under a pump gushing with water. Suddenly her prison walls collapse, the world rushes in, and speech is born for this suffering child. Few more glorious moments exist in world cinema; none evoke more forcefully the impulse of prayer. We rejoice with Helen in the discovery that language carries meaning, that words unite us with all creation, that language is an act of love. With Helen, we instinctively turn to God in adoration, responding to what she describes in *My Religion* (1927) as "the Lord's constant, loving invitation through His Word to all of us, to come Unto Him and choose life."[4]

Orare, Adorare

All people speak and all people pray. (Even our earliest ancestors, to judge by the flowers and other ritual remains unearthed at Pleistocene burial sites, sought communication with the divine.) The Vedic hymns, some of the world's oldest poems, sing of the majesty of the gods, among them Vac, goddess of speech. You might recall, too, that *adorare* means not just "to pray," but "to pray to," to pray toward something—or Someone. Speech and song culminate in prayer, and prayer culminates by turning our face in adoration toward God. And just as speech implies knowledge—a grasp, however tentative, of the meaning embedded in words—so does adoration depend upon knowledge of

God. Coleridge wrote that "in wonder all philosophy began; in wonder it ends . . . but the first wonder is the offspring of ignorance; the last is the parent of adoration." The prayer of adoration, then, includes more than raw amazement at the world (Coleridge's "first wonder"); it includes conscious reflection on God's many splendors.

To understand adoration better and to grasp its implications for our retreat, let us look at "The Call," a poem by George Herbert, whose verses on prayer epitomized the first day of our seclusion:

Come, my Way, my Truth, my Life:
Such a Way as gives us breath:
Such a Truth as ends all strife:
Such a Life as killeth death.

Come, my Light, my Feast, my Strength:
Such a Light, as shows a feast:
Such a Feast, as mends in length:
Such a Strength, as makes his guest.

Come my Joy, my Love, my Heart:
Such a Joy, as none can move:
Such a Love, as none can part:
Such a Heart, as joys in love.5

In this wonderful hymn of adoration, Herbert rejoices in God by calling upon nine divine names: Way, Truth, Life, Light, Feast, Strength, Joy, Love, Heart. These nine names fall neatly into three triads, to each of which Herbert devotes a stanza. The first stanza speaks of Way, Truth, and Life, qualities that define God's sacred being. The second celebrates Light, Feast, and Strength, qualities that define God's glory. The third sings of Joy, Love, Heart, qualities that define God's goodness.

Goodness, glory, sacred being: together, these terms suggest—they can never encompass—the nature of God. As we mull them over, we may notice something remarkable: these things seem to have some connection to our own human attributes of mind, body, and heart. In this three-fold description of God we see ourselves, perfected (Truth as perfection of mind, Strength as perfection of body, Love as perfection of heart). Perhaps we begin to understand that startling, almost scandalous teaching, that human beings have been created in the image and likeness of God. We adore, then, because in God we find ourselves and in ourselves we find God. At the heart of adoration, no less than of *conversio*, lies the mystery of love, which binds us to one another and to God: "God is love, and those who abide in love abide in God, and God abides in them" (1 Jn 4:16).

Adoration ranks as the highest monastic activity, the final aim of *opus Dei*, *lectio divina*, and manual labor. Needless to say, we cannot segregate adoration from the other prayer modes that we have tried out on this retreat. Love inspires them all. We give thanks to God for his gift of love; we petition God because we trust in his love; we praise God as the source of love. Nonetheless, adoration marks a new stage in the life of prayer, a step forward in the monastic path that we assay on this retreat. For just as a child matures by learning to recognize the world as it is in itself rather than simply in reference to himself, in adoration we attain spiritual maturity by shifting focus from ourselves to God. In adoration, then, we marvel, rejoice, glory, bless, stand in acclamation, kneel in amazement, bow in humbleness before God without reservation or restraint.

Adoration is intimately linked to praise, the second of today's prayer themes. We *adore* God as God, the ineffable "I AM WHO I AM" of Exodus. We *praise* God for the gifts of creation, for man and woman, spider and robin, sun and moon, whirlwind and water, the great chain of being unrolled in Genesis. We *praise* creation, both for its intrinsic beauty and goodness and as a palpable sign of God's skillful hand. To those with eyes to see, all creation bears the watermark of God, as William Blake knew well:

> "What," it will be Question'd, "When the Sun rises, do you not see a round disk of fire somewhat like a Guinea?" "O no, no, I see an Innumerable company of the Heavenly host crying 'Holy, Holy, Holy is the Lord God Almighty.' I question not my Corporeal or Vegetative Eye any more than I would Question a Window concerning a Sight. I look thro' it & not with it."[6]

How may we adore and praise on this third day of our retreat? Let us ascend a four-rung ladder, passing through praise of people, art, and nature, to climax in adoration of the Source of all that was, is, or ever will be.

People

Let us praise those whom we love, who staunch our wounds, suffer our stupidities, and champion our cause. Call each beloved to mind as vividly as you can. Praise him, praise her! Praise her small charms, her great gifts, her love for you. What does her presence bring to life in you? How will you greet her when you meet her again? Praise God, in whom all of us "live and move and have our being" (Acts 17:28). Here we discover the indissoluble tie between God and people, for how can I love my beloved (as is commonly said, how can I "adore" her) without loving and adoring the God who made her and sustains her? We glimpse, too, the moral force of praise. For in my beloved, I see all human beings; in her dignity, I find my own. I remember the high state to which I am called. Through praise of others, *conversio* is born.

Art

Let us praise the work of our hands. J.R.R. Tolkien, who knew whereof he spoke, believed that the artist functions as a "subcreator" whose activities reflect—as in a glass, darkly—God's own creation *ex nihilo*. Something of God's creative will flows in our veins and gives life to our arts and artifacts. Not all created things evoke praise; always, moral considerations apply (who would praise an executioner's axe?). But if something displays both intrinsic beauty and a noble purpose, we can be sure that it mirrors the goodness of God.

Almost all common tools fulfill this definition. Examine a hammer, a fork, a pencil. Imagine each item's history—how that hammer began as soil, sun, and air, its head refined from a lump of iron, its handle cut from a hardwood tree. Trace its evolution; bring to mind the innumerable people—miners, farmers, factory workers, sales clerks—who delivered that hammer into your hands. Each of these people has a story to tell, an epic tale that has taken a lifetime to write. Praise them! Think of all the people tied to these hammer-makers as father or mother, sister or brother, cousin, friend, enemy. What better proof of the interconnectedness of all creation? Praise them all! Turn to the hammer's ingenious design, its perfect balance, its appropriate weight (heavy enough to drive a nail, light enough to lift) and shape (front flat for hammering, back split for wrenching). No wonder Thor, mightiest of Norse gods, chose as his emblem the lowly hammer. Praise it!

Let us turn from artifacts to fine art. If you brought an icon with you on retreat, study it now. If not, find a picture on the wall or in a book or in memory, that speaks of God. Scrutinize its color, composition, content. Imagine the artist who stood in front of it. Praise him! Savor the painting's beauty, in which you catch a glimpse of the beauty of God, Maker of its maker. "We have Art that we may not perish from Truth," said Nietzsche. The beauty of sub-creation, no less than the beauty of Creation, reveals the presence of God. Praise all beauty!

Nature

Let us praise the natural world. Nature has been compared to a veil or a mask, cloaking the Divine Face. I'd like to exchange this image for another, a metaphor that emphasizes nature's transparency rather than its opacity: Let us imagine the world as a photographic slide, of infinite extension and immeasurable age, through which shines the light of God. We see a slide by virtue of the light that passes through it, and we see the light by virtue of the images it reveals. Just so, we experience God's light as it shines through the world, and we see the world through the shining of God's light.

How can we be alive to this sense of nature as theophany, the visible presence of God? Sometimes this awareness takes us by surprise: we are rocking in a hammock, adrift in daydreams, when a nuthatch swoops down to snatch a bright red berry, and suddenly we see in that bird, that berry, that glorious swoop, the signature of God. But this appreciation of nature as drenched in God's presence needn't take us by surprise. We can cultivate this faculty. Here, St. Francis can be our tutor; for through his humility and openness to all, Francis became a brother to all sentient beings. Wolves behaved like puppies in his presence; birds ceased their fluttering to listen to his homilies. Anyone who spends much time in the company of animals knows how warmly they respond to human affection: what then of their response to a saint as pure as Francis, to a human love that has become, through a lifetime of *conversio*, a transparency through which shines God's own love?

It's likely that few of us will attain Francis's degree of sanctity, but we can all learn from his example to be more sensitive to God's presence in nature. Walk in garden or woods or along a stream. Pick a pleasant spot, settle down, and examine your surroundings. Consider only a small region, perhaps no more than ten feet square. What do you find here? You may discover your little empire to be crawling with life—arachnids, beetles, worms, or such larger forms as squirrels, mice, voles. Rocks, plants, fungi, soil crowd the scene. Don't forget to look up, into the shaft of air that rises from your tiny plot of land to outer space. What extraordinary airborne beasts, what devious currents of wind, what exotic spores and pollens it contains. Nor should you forget to look down, deep beneath the soil's surface; let your imagination sink, like Jules Verne's intrepid explorers, to the center of the earth.

Now that you have a grasp, however frail, of the staggering intricacies within this snip of territory, choose one aspect of it to meditate upon at length: a dung beetle clambering over a hummock, a rock glistening with mica, a half-crushed daisy. Study this thing that God has made. Sentient or not, it remains a marvel. Befriend it, learn its complexities. Let us suppose that you have chosen a patch of heather. Narrow your attention to one square inch: See how its colors shimmer, break, and coalesce over each millimeter of surface, see how life pulses within it. Learn it, stalk by stalk. Praise it! This exercise gives rise to wonder, and this "wonder born of knowledge" gives birth, as Coleridge says, to adoration.

God

Let us praise and adore God: Father, Son, and Holy Spirit. All things lead to God, for all things come from God. Sun and moon, snails and slugs, our ability to differentiate snails and slugs, our sense of truth, of right, of beauty, all stem from God. According to Christian tradition, life's real aim—no matter how avidly we disguise it or deny it with noisy diversions—is to find, know, and unite with God. Praise for people, craft, art, nature, all come to completion in praise of God. The sign of this, St. Isaac of Syria tells us, is that:

> A man's heart burns for all creation—men, birds, animals, demons, and all creatures. . . . Great and powerful compassion fills a man's heart . . . so that he cannot endure, hear or see any harm or the least pain suffered by a creature. This is why he prays hourly [for] . . . creation . . . with a great compassion which wells up in his heart without measure until he becomes likened in this to God.[7]

What a remarkable idea, to be like God! Yet this extravagant ambition, smacking of hubris, has always been the goal of monasticism and of all Christian life. Notice, however, that Isaac qualifies his statement: we are likened to God in the "great compassion that wells up in our heart without measure." In compassion, in love, in these very human qualities, we find our kinship to God.

Here we must turn to the example of Jesus Christ, both God and man. To whatever degree we "conform ourselves to Christ," as the ancient formula has it, to that extent we follow Isaac's advice to become "likened to God." We arrive at last at the fundamental monastic practice, the struggle to "put on Christ," as Paul puts it, so that "the life of Jesus may be made visible in our mortal flesh" (2 Cor 4:11). In this idea of conformity to Christ, we find the supreme union of our two themes for today, adoration and *conversio*. Through *conversio*, we become likened to that which we adore; we find in ourselves something of the perfect humanity and perfect divinity of Jesus. In rare cases, teach the saints, this process culminates in "divinization" or "deification," the total transformation of the person through union with God. "Those who participate in Him," wrote St. Gregory Palamas, the fourteenth-century exponent of hesychasm (the movement which, you will remember, gave birth to the Jesus Prayer), "will live in a godlike manner, having attained a divine and heavenly form of life."[8]

But what does this lofty teaching mean to us, who are neither monks nor nuns nor saints of any stripe, who struggle every day to get along with our friends, much less love our enemies? Does this extraordinary idea have any practical value on our retreat? I believe it does. Deification can serve us as both goad and goal, a reminder of what we are not and of what we desire to be. Even now, as we slog through the trenches, we can work toward conformity with Christ. In his impeccable life we find, written in flesh and blood, an immaculate map to perfection. For this reason, if for no other, we read the New Testament while on monastic retreat. The daily suggestions for *lectio divina*, the scriptural passages peppered through this book, our private rambles through the gospels, all point us toward Christ's life as the supreme model for our own.

In his brief life—of which we possess so few fragments—one activity recurs so often that it can be called the dominant note against which all others sound. Jesus molds his will to that of the One who sent him: "Not my will but yours be done" (Lk 22:42). His commitment is total; Jesus speaks these words in Gethsemane, in his hour of betrayal, when to champion his own will might have meant escape from crucifixion, perhaps even a long life capped by a distinguished old age. But Jesus surrenders all to God, in an intimacy so great that only the mysterious designations of "Father" and "Son" suffice to describe it:

> Very truly, I tell you, the Son can do nothing on his own, but only what he sees the Father doing; for whatever the Father does, the Son does likewise. . . . As I hear, I judge; and my judgment is just, because I seek to do not my own will but the will of him who sent me. (Jn 5:19, 30)

If, in our work toward *conversio* on this retreat—and during the rest of our lives—deification serves as goal, Jesus as teacher, and his holy life as model, surrender to God's will may serve as our method. In doing so, we join hands with every monk and nun in the world. For, as said above, searching out God's will is the final aim of monastic vocation. Monks and nuns want nothing more than to love; as Father Anselm explained, "The will of God is other people." We celebrate in this great endeavor the final marriage of all the acts and themes of our retreat: of thanksgiving, petition, and adoration; of stability, obedience, and *conversio*; of death, gestation, and resurrection. "Do not be foolish, but understand what the will of the Lord is," says Paul (Eph 5:17), for in so doing we find our bliss: "For this is the will of God, your sanctification" (1 Thes 4:3).

PRAYER PRACTICE
FOR SUNDAY

For twenty centuries, a single prayer has remained at the center of all monastic practice: the Lord's Prayer, delivered by Jesus to his disciples when they asked him, "Lord, teach us to pray." Even today, it remains the best-known prayer in the world. The customary formulation goes:

Our Father who art in heaven,
    hallowed be thy name.
Thy kingdom come, thy will be done,
    on earth as it is in heaven.
Give us this day our daily bread,
    and forgive us our trespasses,
    as we forgive those who trespass against us.
And lead us not into temptation,
    but deliver us from evil.

In this prayer we discern in primordial form each of Jesus' most fundamental teachings, including the primacy of love over hate, forgiveness over vindictiveness, and, above all, the need to unite our will to that of God ("thy will be done on earth as it is in heaven"). In addition, the Lord's Prayer establishes our intimate, even familial relationship to God ("our Father"), proclaims God's holiness ("hallowed be thy name"), petitions God ("give us this day our daily bread"), and humbly asks God to forgive all our faults in light of our forgiveness of others, the reciprocity essential to all real relationships ("forgive us our trespasses, as we forgive those who trespass against us").

On this last day of our retreat, I suggest that we recite the Lord's Prayer silently and at regular intervals, just as we did yesterday with the Jesus Prayer. We will find significant differences between the two prayers. The Lord's Prayer, because of its greater length and complexity, has none of the mantra-like qualities of the Jesus Prayer. It demands a different kind of attention, more fluid, more alert to shifting content. Its life within us will vary accordingly. Let us be sure to listen to each word, to dwell as long as possible on each phrase, each sentence, to soak in the Prayer's liquid rhythms, its stately beauty. At first we may find ourselves drawn to one aspect of the Prayer, perhaps the plea for forgiveness, or the call to do God's will. Later in the day, another phrase may captivate us. Sometimes we will find ourselves wrestling with the significance of a particular word (what did Jesus mean by "Father"?); at other times, we will be dazzled by God's mystery; a little while more, and the various phrases will unite into a luminous whole, and we will say the prayer as if with a single breath. All this is as it should be, for the Lord's Prayer encompasses all prayer, as God encompasses all creation.

A few among us have yet another reason to say the Lord's Prayer: for the difficulties that it may bring. Some people object to all traditional prayers. Why, they ask, don't we compose our own prayers in a contemporary idiom? Why speak of "kingdom" when we inhabit a democracy? Why say "Father" instead of "Creator"? Isn't this a vestige of discarded social views? Others feel bewildered by the plea that God "lead us not into temptation." How can this God who tempts, so reminiscent of the serpent in Eden or the devil assailing Jesus in the wilderness, be at the same time the God of love?

Rather than respond to each of these objections in turn, which would require a tour through the subtleties of biblical translation, Trinitarian theology, philology, religious language, and more, I'd like to lift our discussion to another plane. I ask you to call to mind the monastic attitude that we have tried to cultivate on this retreat, a posture of patience, humbleness, obedience, and love. I will never forget the words that an elderly nun, long experienced in the religious life, addressed to me many years ago in response to my caustic comment about a friend's moral dereliction. She gazed at me kindly for a moment and then said, "In the monastery, we are trained never to judge."

I am still struggling to implement her advice. Nothing cuts against the grain more fiercely, for we judge everything, all the time: the weather, politicians, movies, our lover's face, the thickness of our sandwich. Not to judge! If we could put this wonderful idea into practice, I've little doubt that it would transform the world. But a host of banshees block our way, and the worst of them is habit. Let us pit ourselves against our habits, our reactions, our arrogant certainties. The rewards we reap will be immediate and lasting. Why go on retreat, if not to confront our biases, the easy likes and dislikes that rule our lives, and discover new ways of seeing and doing? Right here, right now, a few of us have a splendid opportunity to quell our ego, to combat our self-love. I urge those with a resistance to the Lord's Prayer to make it their prayer practice for the third day of our retreat.

FINISHING THE DAY

As Sunday draws to a close, we continue the pattern of previous days: twenty minutes of contemplation, followed by Compline and recreation. We should leave our last evening of retreat free of busy work, so that the cumulative effect of three days of solitude can settle into our hearts. Some of us might want to say a special prayer tonight to our chosen saint, asking for heavenly support as we prepare to rejoin the world.

To finish the day, I suggest that we meditate on the following poem by the great Jesuit poet Gerard Manley Hopkins (1844–89), which incorporates so many of the themes (praise, *conversio*, resurrection) that we explored today.

God's Grandeur

The world is charged with the grandeur of God.
    It will flame out, like shining from shook foil;
    It gathers to a greatness, like the ooze of oil
Crushed. Why do men then now not reck his rod?
Generations have trod, have trod, have trod;
    And all is seared with trade; bleared, smeared with toil;

And wears man's smudge and shares man's smell: the soil
Is bare now, nor can foot feel, being shod.
And for all this, nature is never spent;
    There lives the dearest freshness deep down things;
And though the last lights off the black West went
    Oh, morning, at the brown brink eastward, springs—
Because the Holy Ghost over the bent
    World broods with warm breast and with ah! bright
        wings.[9]

chapter 7

Ɛnds and Beginnings

I'll remember forever my first return to the world following a retreat. My solitude had lasted a scant five days,
yet when I quit my refuge—a dilapidated shack edging
its way down a slope on the Vermont–Massachusetts
border—I felt like Robinson Crusoe sailing away from
his island hideaway after twenty-eight years of exile.
Walking toward my car, I drank in the sensations that
rushed my way—the whinny of a horse in a far-away
field, a girl in a blue dress spinning a yellow hoop, the
rank odor of a rotting hayrick. Everything trembled with
inner light; God seemed woven into the landscape, the
sky, the very air.

The first shock came ten minutes later, when I
reached the nearest town and suddenly found myself
in a jigsaw puzzle of clashing colors, screeching cars,
stench and glare, and jostling crowds. I felt dizzy, con-
fused, badly dislocated—all this, mind you, in a village

of less than five thousand souls. I dashed into a nearby supermarket, only to discover there the ninth circle of Hell: row upon row of cans, crates, boxes, bags, bushels, barrels, filled with contents bright and bumpy, wrapped in acres of cardboard, square miles of plastic, a glut beyond imagining—the *sanctum sanctorum* of American consumerism—and every inch plastered with slogans that screamed for attention. My head swam.

Just then a voice called out my name ("God called to him out of the burning bush"). I turned around and saw a dear friend approach. She hugged me, elated at our meeting. Her sweet greeting unlocked my heart. I knew then what St. Benedict meant when he said that "all guests who present themselves are to be welcomed as Christ . . . because he is indeed welcomed in them" (*RB* 53). For I saw in my friend the likeness of the God whom I had sought, prayed to, wept over, befriended during my solitude. I needn't have feared: God had come with me out of the retreat.

Shock will be our inevitable companion as we return to the world, at least during our first years of practice. We can be ready to meet it by planting our feet firmly in God. Grip onto the Lord's Prayer, the Jesus Prayer, or Brother Lawrence's practice of the presence; any of these will lend stability and strength. Remember St. Antony emerging from twenty years of solitude: "He maintained utter equilibrium, like one guided by reason and steadfast in that which accords with nature." Perhaps we can't claim this high state as our own, but we, too, have entered on the path toward equilibrium. For a few days, we have felt the rough, satisfying scratch of the monastic habit against our skins. We have worn it lightly and fleetingly, as befits ordinary men and women on brief monastic retreat. Now we must learn how to wear it in the world.

In this effort, we have a decent head start. We enjoy a beginner's acquaintance with contemplation. We know how prayer can sanctify the day. We have tasted the monastic routines of *opus Dei, lectio divina,* and manual labor, and the monastic vows of stability, obedience, and *conversio.* Our job becomes that of safeguarding these riches from the tarnish of neglect. In order to maintain their luster in our hearts, we must polish them daily, as St. Francis de Sales advises:

> As the birds have nests in the trees that they may have a retreat when they need it . . . so our hearts ought to seek out and choose some place each day . . . near to our Lord, that they may make their retreat on all occasions.[1]

We may be daunted by this challenge. How do we sustain retreat in the midst of the world's hot pawings, not to mention its indifference to the inner life? As a start, I ask you to determine which of the monastic practices covered in this book suit you best. Lock them into your heart. Return to them unflaggingly. Don't let a day go by without some form of prayer. Be ready, whenever you hear the call, to plunge within yourself— whether driving or eating or negotiating a deal—and there offer thanks, petitions, and praise to God. In this gesture we see the true meaning of retreat: not only physical withdrawal from the world (although it is that, to be sure), but an interior disposition grounded in love. As we have learned by now, this loving opening to God can take place in the midst of daily work. "Rejoice always, pray without ceasing, give thanks in all circumstances," writes Paul, "for this is the will of God in Christ Jesus for you" (1 Thes 5:16–18).

I suspect that none of us, during our retreat, heard heavenly hosts shout hosanna, saw fiery chariots streak across the sky, or burned with that strange mystical fire of which the hesychasts write. On the whole, God reserves such gifts for others. What then, came our way? For a few days we left behind our customary activities, we prayed, we read, we worked with our hands. We may not have stormed the land of milk and honey, but perhaps we glimpsed what lies around the next bend in the lifelong path that winds from us to God.

Or perhaps not. Perhaps we learned only to put one foot in front of another, or did no more than to catch our breath before one day—next week? next year?—taking our first real step. This is no mean accomplishment. God rushes to answer our smallest efforts, as Jesus taught: "Ask, and it will be given you; search, and you will find; knock, and the door will be opened for you" (Mt 7:7). In this lovely triple pledge, Jesus assures us of God's courtesy toward all creatures. His promise led us directly to the final theme and the final exercise of our retreat.

If the Divine Office is the monastic prayer *par excellence*, hospitality holds high court among monastic virtues. The Benedictine prepares a place apart—and then opens the door to all who knock. As we have seen, Benedict asks his monks to turn away no one, to welcome everyone as Christ. This gracious activity can be ours as well. The secret of hospitality lies, I believe, in the ability to recognize beauty whenever we meet it. Mother Teresa of Calcutta described her work, which included plucking maggots from the ulcerating limbs of the homeless and dying, as "something beautiful for God." What imparted beauty to her work, she said, was the beauty of those whom she helped. In her eyes, these faces ravaged by disease, poverty, or violence, remained luminous with the presence of God. From this beauty she drew the strength for her impossible task, answering knocks and opening doors on behalf of the "poorest of the poor" twenty-four hours a day.

Beauty works its magic whenever we recognize its knock and let it in. It resurrects us, gives us hope, awakens us to truth, opens us to love. Hospitality is most beautiful, and beauty most hospitable. Let us leave our retreat, then, with a vow of hospitality. Let us welcome whatever comes our way—a dying friend, a reclusive spider, a jewel-encrusted icon, the apothegms of Christ—and find in these gifts the beauty of all created things and of our God, who breathes them into being and upholds them through love.

NOTES

CHAPTER 1

1. Julian of Norwich, *Showings*, trans. Edmund Colledge, O.S.B., and James Walsh, S.J. (New York: Paulist Press, 1978), p. 130.
2. Ralph Waldo Emerson, *The Journals and Miscellaneous Notebooks of Ralph Waldo Emerson*, ed. William H. Gilman, et al. (Cambridge, MA: The Belknap Press of Harvard UP, 1960–84), vol. 7, p. 525.
3. Henry David Thoreau, *Walden and Civil Disobedience*, ed. Michael Meyer (New York: Penguin, 1983), p. 135.
4. Robert Bretall, *A Kierkegaard Anthology* (Princeton, NJ: Princeton University Press, 1946), p. 150.
5. Anthanasius, *The Life of Antony*, trans. Robert C. Gregg (New York: Paulist Press, 1980), p. 42.
6. Saint Augustine, *Confessions*, trans. R. S. Pine-Coffin (London: Penguin Books, 1961), p. 197.

CHAPTER 2

1. Wallace Shawn and Andre Gregory, *My Dinner with Andre* (New York: Grove Press, 1981), p. 96.
2. Denis Huerre, O.S.B., *Letters to My Brothers and Sisters*, trans. Sylvester Houedard, O.S.B. (Collegeville, MN: The Liturgical Press, 1994), p. 22.
3. "The Sayings of the Desert Fathers," in Owen Chadwick, *Western Asceticism* (Philadelphia: Westminster Press, 1958), p. 150.
4. Pope Saint Gregory the Great, *Life and Miracles of St. Benedict*, trans. Odo J. Zimmermann, O.S.B., and Benedict R. Avery, O.S.B. (Collegeville, MN: The Liturgical Press, 1984), p. 12.
5. Denis Huerre, p. 22.

CHAPTER 3

1. Henry David Thoreau, *Collected Essays and Poems*, ed. Elizabeth Hall Witherell (New York: Library of America, 2001), pp. 393–94.

CHAPTER 4

1. Jacques Lusseyran, *And There Was Light*, trans. Elizabeth R. Cameron (Boston: Little, Brown and Co., 1963, reprint ed., New York: Parabola Books, 1987), p. 14.
2. Ibid., p. 16.
3. Ibid., pp. 16–17.
4. Ibid., p. 27.
5. Ibid., 281–3.
6. Ibid., p. 29.
7. Brother Lawrence of the Resurrection, *Writings and Conversations on the Practice of the Presence of God*, Critical Edition by Conrad De Meester, O.C.D., trans. Salvatore Sciurba, O.C.D. (Washington, DC: ICS Publications, 1994), p. 36.

8. George Herbert, *The Complete English Poems* (New York: Penguin, 1991), p. 45.

CHAPTER 5

1. Gilbert Keith Chesterton, *The Man Who Was Thursday: A Nightmare* (New York: Dodd, Mead & Co., 1958), p. 7.
2. Jacques Lusseyran, p. 46.
3. Anonymous, *The Way of a Pilgrim*, trans. R.M. French (2nd edition, New York: Harper, 1954; reprint ed., New York: HarperCollins, 1991), p. 38.
4. Ibid., p. 39.
5. Ronald Stuart Thomas, ed., *The Penguin Book of Religious Verse* (New York: Penguin, 1963), p. 20.
6. Jane Austen, *Catharine and Other Writings*, ed. Margaret Anne Doody and Douglas Murray (New York: Oxford University Press, 1998), p. 249.

CHAPTER 6

1. Quoted in Esther De Waal, *Seeking God* (Collegeville, MN: The Liturgical Press, 1984), p. 70.
2. St. Thérèse of Lisieux, *Story of a Soul*, trans. John Clarke, O.C.D. (Washington, DC: ICS Publications, 1975, 1976), pp. 134–5.
3. Ibid., pp. 276–7.
4. Helen Keller, *My Religion* (Garden City, NY: Doubleday, Page, & Co, 1927), p. 151.
5. George Herbert, p. 147.
6. William Blake, *The Poetry and Prose of William Blake*, ed. David V. Erdman (New York: Doubleday, 1965), p. 555.
7. Quoted in Leonid Ouspensky and Vladimir Lossky, *The Meaning of Icons*, trans. G. E. H. Palmer and E. Kadloubovsky (Crestwood, NY: St. Vladimir's Seminary Press, 1989), pp. 92–3.
8. Quoted in Georgios I. Mantzaridis, *The Deification of Man*, trans. Liadain Sherrard (Crestwood, NY: St. Vladimir's Seminary Press, 1984), p. 22.
9. Gerard Manley Hopkins, *Poems and Prose of Gerard Manley Hopkins*, ed. W. H. Gardner (New York: Penguin, 1985), p. 27.

CHAPTER 7

1. Quoted in John Townroe, "Retreat," in *The Study of Spirituality*, ed. Cheslyn Jones, Geoffrey Wainwright, and Edward Yarnold, S.J. (New York: Oxford University Press, 1986), p. 579.

INDEX

Biblical Index

PHILIP ZALESKI states about himself, "I write and lecture about what I love: faith, spirituality, prayer, the search for God, and how these things play out in our beautiful, fallen culture." He has published four books, most recently *Prayer: A History*, co-authored with his wife Carol Zaleski, with whom he has also written *The Inklings* and *The Book of Hell*, due out in 2010. Philip's essays and book reviews have appeared in *The New York Times*, *First Things, Christian Century*, and *Parabola*. From 1995–2002 he edited the HarperSanFrancisco series The Best Spiritual Writing and soon thereafter became editor of the Houghton Mifflin series The Best American Spiritual Writing. Zaleski is currently a research associate in the Department of Religion at Smith College and resides in western Massachusetts.